Crossway Bible Guide

Series editors: Ian Coffey (NT), Stephen Gaukroger (OT)
Old Testament editor: Stephen Dray

Also in this series
Exodus: Stephen Dray
Leviticus: Derek Tidball
Joshua: Charles Price
Ezra and Nehemiah: Dave Cave
Psalms 1–72: Alan Palmer
Isaiah: Philip Hacking
Mark: David Hewitt
Acts: Stephen Gaukroger
1 Corinthians: Robin Dowling and Stephen Dray
Ephesians: Stephen Motyer
Philippians: Ian Coffey
Timothy and Titus: Michael Griffiths
1 Peter: Andrew Whitman

Dedicated to my wife Trish, without whose encouragement
I would never have written a book.

Haggai, Zechariah and Malachi: Crossway Bible Guide

John James

Crossway Books Leicester

CROSSWAY BOOKS
38 De Montfort Street, Leicester LE1 7GP, England

First published 1996

British Library Cataloguing in Publication Data

A catalogue record for this book is available from the British Library.

ISBN 1-85684-150-2

Set in Palatino

Typeset in Great Britain by Textype Typesetters, Cambridge

Printed in Great Britain by Clays Ltd, St Ives plc

CONTENTS

Welcome!

These days, meeting together to study the Bible appears to be a booming leisure-time activity in many parts of the world. In the United Kingdom alone, it is estimated that over one million people each week meet in home Bible-study groups.

These Bible Guides have been designed to help such groups and, in particular, those who lead them, but they are eminently suitable for individual study. We are also aware of the needs of those who preach and teach to larger groups as well as the hard-pressed student, all of whom often look for a commentary that gives a concise summary and lively application of a particular passage.

We have therefore enlisted authors who are in the business of teaching the Bible to others and are doing it well. They have kept in their sights two clear aims:

1. To explain and apply the message of the Bible in non-technical language.
2. To encourage discussion, prayer and action on what the Bible teaches.

All of us engaged in the project believe that the Bible is the Word of God – given to us in order that people might discover him and his purposes for our lives. We believe that the sixty-six books which go to make up the Bible, although written by different people, in different places, at different times, through different circumstances, have a single unifying theme: That theme is Salvation. This means free forgiveness and the removal of all our guilt, it means the gift of eternal life and it means the wholeness of purpose and joy which God has designed us to experience here and now, all of this being made possible through the Lord Jesus Christ.

How to use your Crossway Bible Guide

These guides have been prepared both for personal study and for the leaders and members of small groups. More information about group study follows on the next few pages.

You can use this book very profitably as a personal study guide. The short studies are ideal for daily reading: the first of the following questions is usually aimed to help you with personal reflection (See *How to tackle personal Bible study*). If you prefer to settle down to a longer period of study you can use three to five studies at a time, and thus get a better overview of a longer Bible passage. In either case using the Bible Guide will help you to be disciplined about regular study, a habit that countless Christians have found greatly beneficial. (See also *How to tackle Haggai, Zechariah and Malachi* for methods of selecting studies if you do not intend to use them all.)

Yet a third use for Crossway Bible Guides is as a quarry for ideas for the busy Bible teacher, providing outlines and application for those giving talks or sermons or teaching children. You will need more than this book can offer of course, but the way the Bible text is broken down, comments offered and questions raised may well suggest directions to follow.

How to tackle personal Bible study

We have already suggested that you might use this book as a personal study guide. Now for some more detail.

One of the best methods of Bible study is to read the text through carefully several times, possibly using different versions or translations. Having reflected on the material it is a good discipline to write down your own thoughts before doing anything else. At this stage the introduction of other books can be useful. If you are using this book as your main study resource, then read through the relevant sections carefully, turning up the Bible references that are mentioned. The questions at the end of each chapter are specifically designed to help you to apply the passage to your own situation. You may find it helpful to write your answers to the questions in your notes.

It is a good habit to conclude with prayer, bringing before God the things you have learned.

If this kind of in-depth study is too demanding for you and you have only a short time at your disposal, read the Bible passage, read the comments in the Bible Guide, think round one of the questions and commit what you have learned to God in a brief prayer. This would take about fifteen minutes without rushing it.

How to tackle your group Bible study

1. Getting help

If you are new to leading groups you will obviously want to get all the help you can from ministers and experienced friends. Books are also extremely helpful and we strongly recommend a book prepared by the series editors of the Crossway Bible Guides specifically for this series: *Housegroups: the leaders' survival guide*: edited by Ian Coffey and Stephen Gaukroger (Crossway Books, 1996). This book surveys the whole range of different types of group, asking what is the point of it all, what makes a good leader, how to tackle your meeting, how to help the members, how to study, pray, share, worship and plenty of other pointers, tips and guidelines.

This book is a 'must' for all leaders of small groups. It is written by a team of people widely experienced in this area. It is available at your local Christian bookshop. If you have difficulty in obtaining a copy write to Crossway Books, Norton Street, Nottingham, NG7 3HR, UK.

2. Planning your programme with a Crossway Bible Guide

This guide is a commentary on God's word, written to help a group to get the most out of their studies. Although it is never ideal to chop up Scripture into small pieces, which the authors never intended, huge chunks are indigestible and we have tried to provide a diet of bite-sized mouthfuls.

If you want to get an overview of the Bible book in a series of meetings you will need to select appropriate studies for each meeting. Read them yourself first and prepare a short summary of the studies you are tackling for your group. Ideally you could write it on a sheet of A5 and hand a copy to each member.

Do not attempt to pack more than one study into one meeting but choose the crucial one, the study which best crystallizes the message. There are examples in *How to tackle Haggai, Zechariah and Malachi* below.

3. Resources

You will find any or all of these books of great value in providing background to your Bible knowledge. Put some of them on your Christmas list and build up your library.

New Bible Dictionary or New Concise Bible Dictionary (IVP)
New Bible Atlas (IVP)
New Bible Commentary (21st Century edition) (IVP)
Everyday Life in Bible Times: John Thompson (IVP)
The Bible User's Manual (IVP)
The Lion Handbook to the Bible (Lion Publishing)
The Message of the Bible (Lion Publishing)
NIV Study Bible (Hodder & Stoughton)
The Bible with pleasure: Stephen Motyer (Crossway Books)

The relevant volume in the IVP Tyndale Commentary series will give you reliable and detailed help with any knotty points you may encounter.

4. Preparing to lead

Reading, discussing with friends, studying, praying, reflecting on life ... preparation can be endless. But do not be daunted by that. If you wait to become the perfect leader you will never start at all. The really vital elements in preparation are:

▶ prayer (not only in words but an attitude of dependence on God, 'Lord, I can't manage this on my own')

▶ familiarity with the study passage (careful reading of the text, the Bible Guide study and any other resource books that throw light on it) and

▶ a clear idea of where you hope to get in the meeting (notes on your introduction, perhaps, recap what was covered at the last meeting, and what direction you hope the questions will take you in – don't force the group to give your answers).

Here is a short checklist for the busy group leader.

Have I prayed about the meeting?
Have I decided exactly what I want to achieve through the meeting?
Have I prepared the material?
Am I clear about the questions that will encourage positive group discussion?
Am I gently encouraging silent members?
Am I, again gently, quietening the chatterers?
Am I willing to admit ignorance?
Am I willing to listen to what the group says and to value their contributions?
Am I ready not to be dogmatic, not imposing my ideas on the group?
Have I planned how to involve the group in discovering for themselves?
Have I developed several 'prayer points' that will help focus the group?

Are we applying Scripture to our experience of real life or only using it as a peg to hang our opinions on?

Are we finding resources for action and change or just having a nice talk?

Are we all enjoying the experience together?

How to tackle Haggai, Zechariah and Malachi

Now let's assume that you are planning an eight-week course of studies (you will have to make the adjustments if you have more or fewer meetings). Where do you begin? This is entirely up to you and your group of course but, to get you started, here are some possible routes you might take:

1. A meal of one book – Malachi

There are seven studies in Malachi. If you have an eight-week course it would be wise to use the section on interpreting the prophets on p. 21ff for the opening meeting of the series.

2. A detailed study of visions

Zechariah 1:7 to 6:8 contains a series of eight visions. This could provide your group with a fascinating in-depth study. You could use part of the first meeting to introduce the three minor prophets (see the comment on Malachi above).

3. Haggai and Malachi

There is not enough material to do a series on Haggai alone. If you want to study this book, either opt for a short five-week course, or six if you do an introduction as suggested above. Alternatively you could take five weeks to study Haggai and add three studies from Malachi to give a flavour of the book, such as Malachi 1:1–5; 2:1–9 and 3:6–12.

These outlines are meant to be springboards for your own ideas, so please do not follow them slavishly. Adapt them for your own use, merge them or ignore them. In any case you will not usually have time to use all of these studies. You, as leader, will need to read the whole of Haggai, Zechariah and Malachi so that you can refer your group to sections they have not read. It would be wise to read aloud a whole chapter whenever studying a part of it – the context often throws light on the verses you are looking at.

What can we expect to learn from Haggai, Zechariah and Malachi?

These three are the last of the Old Testament prophets and they lived and worked in the fifth century BC (the '400s'). They are called 'post-exilic' because their task was to bring God's message of hope and encouragement to his people after they had returned from exile in far away Babylon. We can apply their message to our own situation in a spirit of new and returning life, rebuilding, finding our feet again after a period of being lost. Above all it is a positive note of encouragement for us all.

- Haggai helps us to sort out our priorities as individuals as well as congregations.

- He points to what is wrong in our lives and shows the way to personal renewal.

- Zechariah shows us the coming Messiah and helps us to prepare for his return.

- He reminds us that our best efforts are not enough to accomplish spiritual purposes; '"Not by might, nor by power, but by my Spirit," says the LORD.'

- Malachi looks forward to the return of God to his people and sets before us the reforms that we need in preparation.

- He calls us to abandon lifeless forms of worship and prepare for revival.

- Malachi also points the way to dealing with our financial difficulties.

Finding your way round this book

In our Bible Guides we have developed special symbols to make things easier to follow. Every study therefore has an opening section which is the passage in a nutshell.

The main section is the one that *makes sense of the passage*.

Questions

Every passage also has special questions for personal and group study after the main section. Some questions are addressed to us as individuals, some speak to us as members of our church or home group, while others concern us as members of God's people worldwide. The questions are deliberately designed:

▶ to get people thinking about the passage

▶ to apply the text to 'real life' situations

▶ to encourage reflection, discussion and action!

As a group leader you may well discover additional questions that will have special relevance to your group, so look out for these and note them in your preparation time.

Digging deeper

Some passages, however, require an extra amount of explanation, and we have put these into two categories. The first kind gives additional background material that helps us to understand something factual. For example, if we dig deeper into the gospels, it helps us to know who the Pharisees were, so that we can see more easily why they related to Jesus in the way they did. These background sections are marked with a spade.

Important doctrines

The second kind of explanatory background section appears with passages which have important doctrines contained in them and which we need to study in more depth if we are to grow as Christians. Special sections that explain them to us in greater detail are marked with a face as above.

Historical background to Haggai, Zechariah and Malachi

Judah was situated in the present-day Middle East (see map on p. 19), an area which has seen continual turmoil and conflict as great empires struggled for supremacy and small countries struggled for independence.

The temple of Haggai's prophecy seems to symbolize this struggle. It had been a magnificent structure, built by David's son, Solomon, during his reign (970–930 BC). He was the last king of a united Israel; shortly after his death in 930 BC it was divided into the Northern kingdom of Israel with its capital, Samaria, and the Southern kingdom of Judah, centred on Jerusalem.

Both kingdoms were threatened by neighbouring powers and in this period the mighty Assyrian Empire grew, expanding eastwards. Eventually both Israel and Judah had to submit to Assyria; Israel rebelled and in 722 BC was invaded and its capital Samaria, was destroyed. Part of its population was deported to other parts of the Assyrian Empire, being replaced by foreigners, and Israel ceased to be a kingdom.

Judah continued under Assyrian power but with its own king, until it, too, rebelled. In 701 BC Sennacherib invaded, captured part of its territory and deported some of the population.

In its turn the Assyrian Empire declined and the Babylonian Empire became ascendant. Again Judah rebelled under its king Jehoichin and in 597 BC he and a major part of the population were exiled to Babylon. Subsequently a second rebellion led by Zedekiah against Nebuchadnezzar again failed, Jerusalem was besieged in 587 BC resulting in the destruction of the city and the temple, and its inhabitants were exiled to Babylon. The rule of the kings of Judah ended at this time.

The Babylonian Empire itself declined and was overrun by the Persians. It was the Persian king, Cyrus (559–530 BC) who issued a decree in 538 BC allowing all exiles to return to their own lands and gave permission to the Jews to rebuild their temple at Jerusalem, providing money for them to do so. The first Jews returned to Jerusalem from Babylon in 537 BC.

The events up to the exile are recorded in 1 and 2 Kings and the return from exile and rebuilding of the temple and walls of Jerusalem are recorded in Ezra and Nehemiah (see D. Cave, *Ezra & Nehemiah* (Crossway Books, 1993)).

Time chart

722 BC	The Assyrians destroyed Samaria (Israel, the Northern Kingdom)
701	Sennacherib invaded Judah and deported many of its inhabitants
605	The first deportations of Jews to Babylon began
597	Jehoiachin, King of Judah, and 10,000 men are exiled
587	The temple in Jerusalem is destroyed by Babylonian King Nebuchadnezzar, and more people are deported
539	Cyrus the Persian defeats Babylon
538	Cyrus issues the decree which gives all captives permission to return home
537	The first of God's people return home from captivity
530	Cambyses II becomes ruler of the Persian Empire
522	Darius I becomes emperor
516–15	The temple at Jerusalem is completed
486	Xerxes I becomes emperor – and later Esther is made his queen

464	Artaxerxes I becomes emperor
458	Ezra arrives in Jerusalem
445	Nehemiah arrives in Jerusalem
444	Jerusalem city wall is restored
433	Nehemiah returns to Babylon
?	Nehemiah visits Jerusalem again
423	Darius II rules Persia

Haggai and Zechariah were writing around 520 BC, Malachi about sixty years later.

The Persian Empire, 6th–5th centuries BC

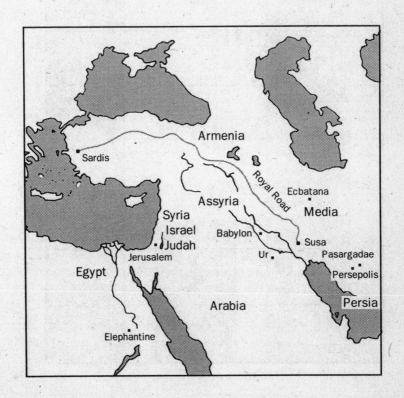

The prophets in their time

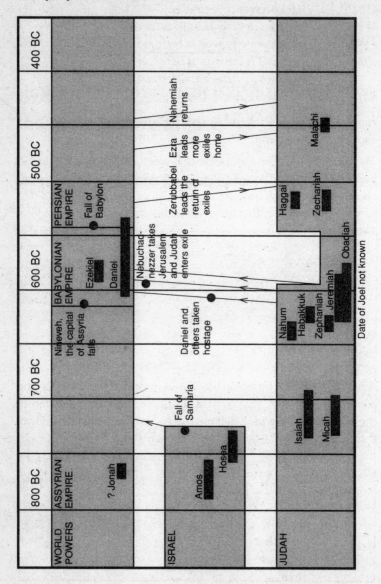

	800 BC		700 BC		600 BC		500 BC		400 BC
WORLD POWERS	ASSYRIAN EMPIRE		Nineveh, the capital of Assyria falls		BABYLONIAN EMPIRE	PERSIAN EMPIRE			
ISRAEL	? Jonah		Fall of Samaria		Daniel and others taken hostage	Fall of Babylon		Nehemiah returns	
	Amos	Hosea			Ezekiel	Daniel	Zerubbabel leads the return of exiles	Ezra leads more exiles home	
					Nbuchad-nezzer takes Jerusalem and Judah enters exile				
JUDAH			Isaiah	Micah	Nahum		Haggai		Malachi
					Habakkuk		Zechariah		
					Zephaniah				
					Jeremiah	Obadiah			

Date of Joel not known

20

Interpreting Haggai, Zechariah and Malachi

The prophets Zechariah and Haggai were called to motivate the people to rebuild the temple in Jerusalem. Zechariah's vision, however, was much broader than the more practical Haggai. He saw God breaking into history on behalf of his people. He looks down the ages and sees the coming of the king, the Messiah, who establishes his everlasting kingdom.

For the Christian, the book of Zechariah has special worth, because the New Testament throws light on it as containing tremendous testimony to the person and work of Jesus Christ. Zechariah's prophecies speak of Jesus as king, shepherd and sufferer, who ushers in the end time, establishes the Messianic kingdom and fulfils in himself the promise of God and the hope of Israel.

More than any other of the minor prophets he foretells the coming of Jesus (3:8; 9:9, 16; 10:11; 13:7). He speaks of the blood of the covenant (9:11) and the betrayal of Judas (11:12–13). He predicts the conversion of Israel to the Lord (12:10) and their cleansing through the fountain opened by the Messiah's death on Calvary (12:10; 13:1), and he predicts the final day of the Lord (14:1ff).

Sometimes however, you look at an event in the New Testament in which the writer has claimed the fulfilment of Old Testament prophecy and you wonder why that verse has been applied to that situation for it doesn't always seem to fit.

On all such occasions remember, 'Above all, you must understand that no prophecy of Scripture came about by the prophet's own interpretation. For prophecy never had its origin in the will of man, but men spoke from God as they were carried along by the Holy Spirit' (2 Peter 1: 20–21).

Therefore, when we come to interpret Scripture, we need to pray for the inspiration of the Holy Spirit. The Spirit that inspired prophets before Christ, and inspired the New Testament writers in their understanding of it, is the same Holy Spirit who is available to help us in our understanding and interpretation of Scripture.

The use of Old Testament prophecies in the New Testament

When the gospel writers came to record the events of the life, the death and resurrection of Jesus, there was no doubt in their minds it was all according to Scripture.

After the resurrection, Jesus met two disciples on the Emmaus road, 'and beginning with Moses and all the Prophets, he explained to them what was said in all the Scriptures concerning himself' (Luke 24:27). Later, talking to the disciples, he said, 'Everything must be fulfilled that is written about me in the Law of Moses, the Prophets and the Psalms' (Luke 24:44).

There are at least four ways in which the disciples quote the Old Testament prophecies.

1. Literal prophecy and literal fulfilment

This is where the original prophecy was spoken and fulfilled. In Zechariah 9:9 Zion's King is predicted riding into Jerusalem, 'gentle, and riding on a donkey'. Matthew, in recording the triumphal entry, has no hesitation in saying that Zechariah had already said that this was going to happen. Another illustration is found in Micah 5:2 where Bethlehem Ephrathah is announced as the birthplace of the Messiah. The scribes were expecting it and sent the wise men to search him out: the literal prophecy with a literal fulfilment.

2. Literal and typical prophecy

This is where the original prophecy related to a literal situation, perhaps in the immediate future, but also was to act as a type or symbol. In Zechariah 13:7 we read, 'Strike the shepherd and the sheep will be scattered'. To Zechariah's congregation Jehovah was their shepherd and this would have been understood as saying, 'If Jehovah's people rebelled against him they would suffer'. Look, however, at Matthew 26:31 and we read of Jesus, talking to his disciples, and he takes these very words from Zechariah and shows that the prophecy also serves as a type of him. Then Jesus told them, 'This very night you will all fall away on account of me, for it is written, "I will strike the shepherd and the sheep of the flock will be scattered".' To use another illustration compare Hosea 11:1 and Matthew 2:15: 'Out of Egypt I called my son.' In Hosea's mind, originally, there is no doubt that he would have been thinking of Israel, God's son, literally called from Egypt. Matthew sees it as a type of Jesus who, as an infant, was a refugee in Egypt and returned to Israel after Herod's death (Matthew 2:13–21). Here is a dual use of prophecy, literal and typical.

3. Literal and applied prophecy

See Zechariah 11:12, 'So they paid me thirty pieces of silver.' The literal understanding is that the prophet was paid as a slave for doing the work of a shepherd – exploitation. Compare Matthew 27:10 and the gospel writer applies the prophecy to the thirty pieces of silver paid to Judas Iscariot when he betrayed Jesus to the priests. A second illustration of this use is seen by comparing Jeremiah 31:15 with Matthew 2:17–18. Jeremiah referred to the women of Judah who mourned their children as they were taken to Babylon, but Matthew applies it to Herod's infanticide at the birth of Jesus. Here is another dual use of prophecy, literal and applied.

4. Summary use of prophecy

The fourth way in which the New Testament writers quote the Old Testament prophet is seen in Matthew 2:23 and is in the form of a summary. 'He [Jesus] went and lived in a town called Nazareth. So was fulfilled what was said through the prophets: "He will be called a Nazarene".' Notice Matthew said, prophets – plural. Yet nowhere can you find an Old Testament prophet recording this form of words. So why did Matthew say it? Well, what is a Nazarene? That's clear enough from the Old Testament. It is someone who is despised and rejected by men. What did many of the prophets say about the coming of the Messiah? That he would be despised and rejected by men. So Matthew is summarizing what the Old Testament prophets said.

Now in understanding prophecy we need to keep these principles very much in mind. To benefit most from the study of the prophetic Scriptures it is important to keep in mind the following principles for interpretation.

i. Acknowledge the authority of the prophets. Remember how the Lord Jesus never doubted their authority. Through them the Lord made known the truth about the future.

ii. As a normal rule, the prophecies should be interpreted literally unless the content of the Scriptures or common sense indicate otherwise.

iii. Remember holy Scripture is rich with metaphors, figures of speech, symbols and types. We have to use God-given common-sense as we interpret the text in its context.

iv. Recognize the value of God's progressive revelation. Later writings in the Bible often explain that which was written earlier. Examples of this are noted above when we observed how New Testament writers interpreted Old Testament prophecy.

v. Distinguish between that which the prophets said to their own day and that which has a future relevance, observing the difference between forth-telling and fore-telling. Sometimes as above, the prophecy applied to something imminent and distant.

vi. Remember to keep prophecy in a proper relationship with the rest of Scripture. Don't read into Scripture what is not there. It is important that Christ and the total message of the Bible be kept in mind at all times.

vii. Ensure that we compare Scripture with Scripture. We must then interpret details in the light of the entire Word of God.

HINDRANCES TO RESTORATION

Haggai 1:1 – 2:9

Haggai 1:1–15

Forgetting who comes first

We are to give God first place in our lives.

The exiles had begun to return to Jerusalem from Babylon and were charged to build the temple. The background to the return is provided by Ezra in chapters 1 – 6. Haggai prophesied in 520 BC, sixteen years after Zerubbabel had led the first party of exiles back to Jerusalem. Sixteen years had passed and still no temple. That is the problem Haggai is facing. When the exiles first returned there was initial enthusiasm and in 537 BC they had re-established temple worship by consecrating the altar. The temple itself was a mass of rubble, still as it was when the Babylonians destroyed it fifty years before. They had tried to restore it, but opposition and apathy had brought the work to a standstill (Ezra 4:4–5). For years nothing had been done and so Haggai and Zechariah had begun to motivate them (Ezra 5:1–2). The temple was ultimately completed in 516 BC, seventy years after its destruction – just as Jeremiah had predicted.

The excuses we make

The exiles said 'The time has not yet come for the LORD's house to be built' (1:2). Their duty was to build. They had known it for a long time, but they were saying that it wasn't time. It is easy for us to understand this attitude, we adopt it regularly. We like saying that this needs to be done, but not yet, let's leave it a while, until tomorrow or next week or next year. We understand, for many of us are just like that.

St Augustine in the fourth century AD, running away from his conscience, is said to have prayed, 'God give me grace, but not yet'.

The challenge we need to face

In his reply, Haggai makes a threefold contrast; a contrast of persons, houses and conditions (1:4). In the contrast of persons, God, whose house is in ruins, is not named, but they are. Notice the double emphasis on 'You yourselves'. He was reminding them of who they were, the people of God, who had a remarkable history, with a personal knowledge of God and a clear understanding of the importance of the temple. In contrasting the houses, 'Your houses' with 'this house', Haggai is referring to the places where they lived as families and God's house, the place appointed for their meeting as family with God. In contrasting the conditions, they lived in 'panelled houses' which means expensive, luxury homes. Today these would be detached, centrally-heated, double-glazed homes. The people had feathered their own nests well. In contrast, God's house was a ruin, overgrown with weeds; God was living in a lean-to and they were in luxury.

The tragedy of failure to seek God first

Now Haggai draws their attention to their recent material and financial set-backs. 'You have planted much, but have harvested little. You eat, but never have enough. You drink but never have your fill. You put on clothes, but are not warm. You earn wages, only to put them in a purse with holes in it' (1:6). They had become materialistic again so God spoke to them through their problems. At least that is what is implied. It may have been intended to be understood in spiritual rather than material terms. But the end of verse 6 is a wonderful way of describing inflation. Life was very hard with food shortages, with prices soaring and all because people had their priorities wrong. Everyone was wrapped up in their own selfish concerns and God was neglected. Consequently the very things people wanted were missed. All the good things of life are God's to give or withhold.

It is at this point that we need to emphasize that this is not prosperity theology being proved in reverse. We reject that doctrine as unbiblical and cruel to the poor of the world whose Christian commitment often puts the shallowness of Western Christianity to shame.

The truth being expressed was put like this by the Lord Jesus, 'Seek first his kingdom and his righteousness, and all these things will be given to you as well' (Matthew 6:33). In the context of this verse, our Lord was saying that we should not worry about things: things to eat, drink or wear *etc.*; rather we are to concentrate on him, his will and his righteousness, for he can be trusted to provide all that is necessary to meet our needs. God will not have our hearts fixed on material things. He wants our gaze fully focused on himself. There is nothing wrong with possessing wealth, provided it is held in trust for God and we see ourselves as just stewards of the Lord's possessions.

When as Christians we feather our own nest without a sense of spiritual priorities, we can expect the Lord to come and stir and shake us out of our selfishness. 'Whoever prays for wealth for its own sake' says a Welsh proverb, 'is like a man who drinks sea water; the more he drinks the more he thirsts and he ceases not to drink until he perishes.'

Other applications that could be made are endless, in national, social, congregational and individual lives. Wherever we put things before people and people before God, we are in error.

Haggai's words strike home to the nation's conscience. His authority is recognized and repentance follows, which brings its own fruit of encouragement. '"I am with you", declares the LORD' (1:13). They find their enthusiasm rekindled and within three weeks the work on the temple is resumed.

Questions

1. What excuses have you used for delaying God's will in your life?
2. What do you think happens when the church ignores God's instruction?
3. Haggai argued that life was hard, food in short supply and prices soaring – all because their priorities were wrong. He promises if they put God first all of these adverse circumstances would be reversed. Does it sound like the 'prosperity' doctrine to you? What do you make of it?

Personalities

King Darius (verse 1). This is Darius the first ruler of the Persian Empire (522–486 BC) and not to be confused with Darius the Mede mentioned in the book of Daniel (Daniel 6:6, 9, 25). The name means 'he who sustains good thought'. He became king after the death of Cambyses, but not before two others tried to take the throne first. It was this king who allowed the Jews, who had returned, to build the temple in accordance with the decree of Cyrus (Ezra 1:2–4; 5:1 – 6:15).

Zerubbabel (verse 1) probably means 'Seed of Babylon' or 'born in Babylon' and he was the grandson of Jehoiachin (Ezra 3:2; Matthew 1:12–13). He returned with Sheshbazzar in 537 BC in order to rebuild the temple and is normally associated with Joshua the high priest.

Joshua (verse 2). He is not to be confused with the Joshua who led the Israelites into the promised land, but he was a descendant from the last chief priest Jehozadak (1 Chronicles 6:15), and was probably made high priest at Jerusalem as a result (Zechariah 3:1). In Aramaic the name for Joshua is Jesus and Jesus would have been known as Joshua by his family.

Haggai 2:1–9

Remembering the good old days

Remembering the good old days can have a devastating effect on morale when things are not going well today. Haggai calls for obedience and gives words of encouragement to the people.

Haggai's reference to dates here is very significant; compare 1:1; 1:15 and 2:1. Time is flying by and despite the urgency of the prophet's message and the apparent willing-
ness to begin the work, the people seem to be dragging their feet. What could account for the delay?

During these dates, the Day of Atonement and the following Festival of Tabernacles would have taken place. Such festivals find the Hebrews engaging in what they like doing best, looking back and re-living their history. This is the context in which we find the prophet reminding them of two truths.

The comparison of the temples (2:3)

'Who of you is left who saw this house in its former glory?
How does it look to you now? Does it not seem to you like
nothing?' (2:3)

Ezra provides the answer: 'Many of the older priests and Levites
and family heads, who had seen the former temple, wept aloud
when they saw the foundations of this temple being laid, while
many others shouted for joy' (Ezra 3:12). They could remember
the glory of the past temple and the comparative inferiority of
the new construction disheartened them. It seemed as nothing.
Solomon's temple was tremendous. Not all had seen it, but
everyone had heard of it. None of the glory had been lost in the
telling.

You can imagine the tension; the young people wanting a
functional building now, whereas the older folk who can
remember the splendour of Solomon's temple are prepared to
wait as long as necessary to get it right. There is of course, the
third group, those who have never believed in the building
project anyway. They believe that the delay is divine
confirmation of their point of view. For those of us that have
been involved in rebuilding projects it has a certain
contemporary ring about it.

Living and ministering as I do in the principality of Wales,
this former land of revivals, this passage is so relevant. The
saints still remember the glory of the good old days, with
chapels full, at least for Sunday school anniversary and singing
festivals! And now today, even with occasional new work, it
seems as nothing. To the people of his day and to us, Haggai
comes to encourage us with the second truth.

The covenant of the Lord (2:4–5)

'But now be strong, O Zerubbabel,' declares the LORD. 'Be
strong, O Joshua son of Jehozadak, the high priest. Be strong,
all you people of the land,' declares the LORD, 'and work. For I

am with you,' declares the LORD Almighty. 'This is what I covenanted with you when you came out of Egypt. And my Spirit remains among you. Do not fear.' (2:4–5)

In effect, the message is, take courage in hand, discover what God wants you to do and yield to him the obedience of faith. Don't be daunted by the significant past or by the size of the present task. Prove now the obedience of your faith and do the work. It is enough to know that the covenant-keeping God is with you.

Having proved his faithfulness the Lord makes a further promise.

This is what the LORD Almighty says: 'In a little while I will once more shake the heavens and the earth, the sea and the dry land. I will shake all nations, and the desired of all nations will come, and I will fill this house with glory,' says the LORD Almighty. 'The silver is mine and the gold is mine,' declares the LORD Almighty. 'The glory of this present house will be greater than the glory of the former house,' says the LORD Almighty. 'And in this place I will grant peace,' declares the LORD Almighty. (2:6–9)

The phrase 'In a little while I will once more ...' (2:6) must be understood as a prophetic phrase. Peter writing much later reminds us that we must not forget that 'With the Lord, a day is like a thousand years and a thousand years are like a day' (2 Peter 3:8).

Haggai is engaging in foretelling the future. They are to see the present building as just a foretaste of the glory of the end times, the era of peace and prosperity to which the prophet was looking forward. He encourages them to look beyond the building of this temple to an event that is to be truly earth-shattering, something that will 'Shake the heavens and the earth, the sea and the dry land'. This prophecy found partial fulfilment in the first coming of our Lord Jesus. Many commentators believe 'the desired of all nations' speaks of Jesus. In Hebrews 12:25–29 this passage is quoted and is clearly related to both the first and second comings of our Lord Jesus.

Certainly our Lord Jesus graced the temple courts with his glory during his earthly ministry and John wrote, 'We have seen his glory, the glory of the One and Only, who came from the Father, full of grace and truth' (John 1:14). It has therefore been partially fulfilled, but the final stage is still awaited. Until that final day, realizing the presence of the Spirit, we must continue to prove our obedience by completing the task of building the Kingdom.

Questions

1. What responsibility has God placed on you personally in the work of the Kingdom? How do you respond when volunteers are asked for in your local church?
2. In what ways can we encourage one another to be obedient in the work of God?
3. In the worldwide church today, how would you say it compared to the church of the New Testament? What are the differences and the similarities?

The promises of God

Through Haggai's prophecy God made five promises to the Israelites:

▶ His presence to strengthen (2:4–5)

▶ His power to shake (2:6–7)

▶ His glory to fill (2:7)

▶ His resources to provide (2:8)

▶ His peace to come (2:9).

35

Dates

The four messages of Haggai are delivered over a four-month period. The first is dated the first day of the sixth month (1:1). This is the Hebrew month 'Elul' and is equivalent to our August and September. The second message was delivered on the twenty-first day of the seventh month (2:2). This is the Hebrew month 'Tishri' and is equivalent to our September and October. The third and fourth messages were delivered on the same day, the twenty-fourth day of the ninth month (2:10 and 2:20), that is, the Hebrew month 'Kislev' and is equivalent to November and December.

The Jewish calendar is based on the phases of the moon, and so each month lasts twenty-eight days. When the calendar becomes a month out, the extra month of 'Adar' is added and the month always begins with the new moon.

THE PROMISE OF
RESTORATION

Haggai 2:10-23

Haggai 2:10–19

Strange questions

God's blessings do not depend on our deserving them – but they do have to be received.

Haggai's third message is approached through a dialogue with the priests, the whole point of which is to remind God's people that working on the temple must not be seen as a way of scoring credit points with the Lord. God's blessing is independent of merit. Notice the two questions.

A question of consecration

This is what the LORD Almighty says: 'Ask the priests what the law says: If a person carries consecrated meat in the fold of his garment, and that fold touches some bread or stew, some wine, oil or other food, does it become consecrated?' The priests answered 'No'. (2:11–12)

'Consecrated meat' was the meat of sacrifice. Although the garment had become consecrated, it had no power to transmit holiness any further. The principle is that a holy act cannot consecrate an unsanctified person or thing, by any inherent efficacy of its own. Personal application to the priest and consecration on the altar must be present. In other words, their work, no matter how religious, could not avail in terms of making a person holy. The people were engaged on holy business, building a temple, but the holiness of the task had no way of making them holy.

How often do we consciously or unconsciously try to impress the Lord by what we do for him? Consecration to the Lord himself must come before the service that we render to him. In New Testament language, 'I urge you, brothers, in view of God's mercy, to offer your bodies as living sacrifices, holy and pleasing to God – this is your spiritual act of worship . . . Then you will be able to test and approve what God's will is – his good, pleasing and perfect will' (Romans 12:1–2).

Only the bringing of our very lives to the altar of the New Testament – the cross of our Lord Jesus Christ – can make us holy. As the second verse of the hymn 'Rock of Ages' puts it,

Not the labours of my hands
Can fulfil Thy laws demands:
Could my zeal no respite know,
Could my tears forever flow,
All for sin could not atone;
Thou must save and Thou alone.

A. M. Toplady

A question of contamination

Then Haggai said, 'If a person defiled by contact with a dead body touches one of these things, does it become defiled?'

'Yes', the priests replied, 'it becomes defiled.'

Then Haggai said, 'So it is with this people and this nation in my sight,' declares the LORD. 'Whatever they do and whatever they offer there is defiled' (2:13–14).

This question put to the priest is the other side of the same coin. The people thought that their outward performance ought to

39

have consecrated them and secured the blessing of God. But they were wrong, for by the first illustration we see they have no power to do so and by the second their service was defiled by what they were. The principle is plain, only a personal relationship with God and faith in him is accounted as righteousness. Their moral corruption could undermine the integrity and holiness of the temple that they were building.

Haggai is emphasizing the need for moral integrity to accompany ritual integrity. God's people were engaged in holy work and, as such, their lives needed to live up to their calling. Failure to do so would undermine the very work in which they were engaged. The temptation that faces us all engaged in God's work, is to think that what we do for God will cover up the sin in our lives. The lesson is clear, when we seek to serve God we must watch the state of our heart. Otherwise we face the danger of contaminating God's work.

The rest of this passage is a word of consolation (verses 15–19). If their hearts are right with God, the Lord will take away the judgment of famine, which they were now to understand as chastening, and from this very day their fortunes were to be restored.

Haggai asked the people to 'give careful thought' to the situation that prevailed before the rebuilding work had commenced. Three times he uses this phrase in verses 15–18 and it is a repetition of the truth emphasized in his first message (1:2–11). Throughout that period of misplaced priorities, right up to the date that they resumed the work of restoration, their harvest had been a disappointment. The explanation is now forthcoming. '"I struck all the work of your hands with blight, mildew and hail, yet you did not turn to me", declares the LORD.'

What a challenge: while we take no care of God's interests why should he take care of ours?

God disciplines us through all the events of life, because he loves us (see Hebrews 12:6) and always his motive is to bring us to a place of blessing.

40

To my mind, the key verse for the understanding of Haggai's prophecy is verse 19. 'Is there yet any seed left in the barn? Until now, the vine and the fig tree, the pomegranate and the olive tree have not borne fruit. From this day on I will bless you' (2:19).

Materially and spiritually God's people were impoverished. This was not his desire, which was to bless his people, but they needed to move into a position where they could receive the blessings. What does the Bible mean when it says, 'God will bless us'?

I believe this is a principle and concept that is little understood by Christians today. In both the Old and the New Testaments, the blessing of God implies a right relationship with God.

> The matter of our relationship with God is of supreme importance. I saw an amusing cartoon some time ago: it showed a poor beggar on a street corner clothed in rags and tatters, and a policeman was saying,
>
> 'Now then, move on! What are you looking so miserable about?'
>
> The beggar replied, 'Andrew Carnegie, the millionaire is dead.'
>
> 'What is that to you, was he a relative of yours?'
>
> 'No', said the beggar, 'that's why I am weeping!'
>
> It was all a matter of relationship, to be in a right relationship with God means to be rich. We may all be spiritual millionaires. We do not now use the phrase, 'Get right with God' as we used to; but nevertheless, it is the very key to the spiritual life.
>
> A. Lindsey Clegg, *Life with a capital 'L'*

To be blessed by God is to know the good things of God. It is to know a touch from God that brings life and transforms situations. It is to know the grace – the undeserved favour of God – influencing every area of our lives.

The grace of God flows like a river towards undeserving people, and if we are to be blessed, we have to be in its flow. If we are to be filled by the grace of God, we must be in vital touch with him and obedient every step of the way. The trouble with many of us is that we are out of touch with God and consequently there is no blessing.

When I was a small lad, we lived in a family house with a yard and garage to the rear. The owner rented out the garage to various car owners. The garage had a sloping corrugated roof without any rainwater guttering. It had been a very dry summer, with a drought, and severe water restrictions were in force. Weather forecasts predicted heavy rainfall at night. My father therefore, put the old zinc bath, buckets and bowls in place to catch any cascading water from the garage roof. Unfortunately, one of the garage tenants came along, after they had been strategically placed and, not realizing why they were there, pushed them aside to garage his car. It did rain, but none of the water found its way into the receptacles!

That is the picture of many Christian lives. They are not in the right place, not in a right relationship with God and therefore miss the blessings.

Haggai's call is a call for a change of mind and gives God's promise that the next season's harvest will be marked by blessing, not curse. The day on which he was prophesying was a day that would mark a turning point in Judah's fortunes because the conditions were now in place for the experience of divine blessing.

Questions

1. List and discuss some of the wrong motives we have for serving the Lord.
2. The church of Jesus Christ often goes through barren and fruitless times. What lessons can be learned from this passage which might encourage us?
3. What evidence is there to support a claim that the world-wide church is knowing times of blessing today?

Blessings for a defiled people

This is the way in which this section is headed in the New International Version of the Bible. It is a helpful way to describe this passage. It emphasizes Haggai's understanding of Jehovah as a God of mercy and compassion, ready to bless even a defiled people. Even though it be unclean in everything that it does and every offering that it brings, if the nation will repent and respond to God's call, then it will find him willing to bless.

Also pre-eminent in the teaching of Haggai is the thought that we are responsible in life and ultimately accountable to the Lord whose prerogative is the execution of justice in the ordinary events of life. Many see no connection whatever between the way that they live and the material experiences of life. But Haggai challenges such ignorance by proclaiming a direct link between them.

Haggai 2:20–23

Shaking, taking and making!

God's Anointed King is coming again.

Twice in these four verses Haggai is reminded by God that this promise is to be delivered personally to Zerubbabel, the governor of Judah. The people may be interested to understand why they have suffered bad harvests and encouraged to hear of the imminent blessings of a bumper crop, but Zerubbabel has got something else on his mind.

Zerubbabel, the governor, born of King David's line and heir apparent should the throne of Israel be re-established, is clearly thinking about something else. 'What about these world powers and the authority that they wield over us?' He wants to know if the royal line will ever be revived.

To Zerubbabel the promise of this prophecy comes like music to his ears. Three elements of this promise stand out boldly in these verses; 'I will shake' (verse 20); 'I will take' (verse 23); and 'I will make' (verse 23). That the shaking, taking and making are linked together is plain by the phrase, 'On that day,' which reveals that these things will happen simultaneously.

God's promise to shake

I will shake the heavens and the earth. I will overturn royal thrones and shatter the power of the foreign kingdoms. I will overthrow chariots and their drivers; horses and their riders will fall, each by the sword of his brother (2:21–22).

This is typical prophetic language, describing the dawning of a new age in the purposes of God. God repeats the earlier promise (2:6) of a global shake-up. He assures them that they need not be afraid of the extinction of their national sovereignty. They were protected by the eternal God. That is the significance of the second and third elements of the prophecy.

God's promise to take and to make

'On that day,' declares the LORD Almighty, 'I will take you, my servant Zerubbabel son of Shealtiel,' declares the Lord, 'and I will make you like my signet ring, for I have chosen you,' declares the LORD Almighty (2:23).

Zerubbabel was chosen to be taken and made like Jehovah's

'signet ring'. The signet ring is the symbol of executive power, for it was the impression of the ring that sealed the royal authority on documents issued in the king's name. This promise also reverses the specific judgment on Zerubbabel's grandfather Jehoiachin, recorded in Jeremiah 22:24. This reversal is confirmed by the specific pronouncement that Zerubbabel is God's chosen servant for this present task. Zerubbabel was already active in rebuilding the temple and this was the assurance of God's approval and blessing. He was given great success.

The real significance of this prophecy lies at this very point. Before the fall of Jerusalem to Nebuchadnezzar, the future of the chosen people had been linked to the continuity of David's line. The experience of Babylon had changed many people's expectations. For many it would be enough just to get back to the promised land, even if it meant being a colony of the Persian Empire. The prospect of a king, of David's line, had faded from much of their thinking.

Haggai proclaims restoration of land and lineage; of temple and throne. Jehovah had spoken. He will shake and destroy all false authority and power and he will also take and make his chosen one and establish true authority.

God's promise to shake, take and make, must be understood as looking forward to the end times, when Messiah will come and reign.

Zerubbabel is seen as the focus of royalist expectations. In fact he was never crowned, but the prophet was bearing testimony to a hope that refused to die. Messiah would come and how!

The fulfilment of this prophecy as all Messianic prophecies, is found in our Lord Jesus Christ. He is Jehovah's servant. He is owned as God's chosen. Compare Isaiah 42:1 with 1 Peter 2:4 and notice that he is the head of the chosen remnant and in him all believers are chosen.

Our Lord Jesus is also Jehovah's signet ring, for all authority and power is given to him and flows from him.

Then Jesus came to them and said, 'All authority in heaven and on earth has been given to me. Therefore go and make disciples of all nations, baptising them in the name of the Father and of the Son and of the Holy Spirit, and teaching them to obey everything I have commanded you. And surely I am with you always, to the very end of the age.' (Matthew 28:18–20)

How the world has been shaken in our own day and with it the church of Jesus Christ. The prophecy of Haggai and this promise is to us, that though we have been shaken, we will be strong again (Haggai 2:4), because God will rebuild his house and fill it with his promised glory (2:9).

The question comes through the centuries to us, have we kept the vision clear? Do we really believe that God is committed to a glorious church? Do we believe that the Messiah will come again? Do we believe that between the two comings of Christ he has given to us authority to reign in his name.

Questions

1. This passage was a personal word from God to an individual. How does God speak to us personally today?
2. What authority has God given to the church and what does your local church seem to be doing with it?
3. What evidence can you see of a global shake-up taking place and what significance do you believe should be attached to it?

The day of the Lord

'On that day' (2:23). This phrase has significance in the context of the Old Testament prophets. Many of them refer to a distant day of the Lord, which would be one of final judgment, leading to the establishing of the unshakeable kingdom of God.

All of this is echoed in the New Testament. We can best understand the 'day of the LORD' in Kingdom terms. The Kingdom of God has come, is daily established, but still awaits its final consummation.

The Lord Jesus spoke of the 'day of the Son of Man' in very similar terms.

> Once having been asked by the Pharisees when the Kingdom of God would come, Jesus replied, The kingdom of God does not come with your careful observation, nor will people say, "Here it is", or "There it is," because the kingdom of God is within you.'
>
> Then he said to his disciples, 'The time is coming when you will long to see one of the days of the Son of Man, but you will not see it. Men will tell you, "There he is!" or "Here he is!" Do not go running off after them. For the Son of Man in his day will be like the lightning, which flashes and lights up the sky from one end to the other. But first he must suffer many things and be rejected by this generation.' (Luke 17:20–25).

Amid all that is difficult to understand in New Testament prophecy, one thing is clear. All the writers expected at some unknown time the 'parousia', or second coming of Jesus Christ, which will herald in the final day of the LORD. It will be a day when Jesus Christ will be revealed, and is . . . variously called 'the day of our Lord Jesus Christ' (1 Corinthians 1:8); 'the day of the Lord' (1 Corinthians 5:5; 2 Thessalonians 2:2); 'the day of the Lord Jesus' (2 Corinthians 1:14); and 'the day of Christ' (Philippians 1:10, 2:16). It will be a day that will take people unawares, like a thief in the night (1 Thessalonians 5:2; 2 Peter 3:10) ushering in a demon inspired battle, or rather campaign (Revelation 16:14) and finally global destruction (2 Peter 3:12).

Whilst we still confidently await this day of the Lord, we believe that every day is the Lord's. Joel was the so-called minor prophet who emphasized 'The day of the LORD' more than any of the other Old Testament prophets. His teaching was radical. He predicted that the Holy Spirit would be poured out on all

47

flesh (Joel 2:28). He foresaw a day when God's Spirit would be poured out, not just on priests and prophets, but on ordinary people, regardless of sex, age or class.

Gloriously fulfilled and recorded for us in Acts 2 – Peter can cite Joel 2 and interpret the experiences of Pentecost in the light of prophetic fulfilment. We still live in this 'day of the LORD'. Pentecost is still with us. The kingdom has come and we extend its borders. The promise is partially realized, but its fulfilment is still future; we have a deposit guaranteeing its ultimate fulfilment (Ephesians 1:14). We have acquired many of the blessings of the 'day of the LORD,' but we await its glorious consummation, the second coming of Jesus Christ our Lord.

THE SUMMONS
TO REPENT

Zechariah 1:1–6

Zechariah 1:1–6

Repent!

Zechariah's simple message: get right with God.

Zechariah was a contemporary of Haggai. They were working together, encouraging the people to continue the work of restoring the temple in Jerusalem. This was not just putting up a building, but putting worship back at the centre of the redeemed community (Ezra 5:1).

The date given, 'The eighth month of the second year of Darius' (1:1) or October–November 520 BC, is helpful in that it identifies the fact that the work of restoration was already under way (Ezra 4:2), having started two months earlier (Haggai 1:15).

Zechariah was called to preach 'The word of the Lord' (1:1). In his first message he reviewed their past with the clear intention of warning them. He reminded the people that Jehovah had been very angry with their forefathers and warned them not to make the same mistakes. Haggai encouraged the people by looking forward to the glory to come, whereas Zechariah exhorted them by looking back to a past of disobedience.

The prophet had a twofold message; remember the past and return to the Lord.

Remember the past (1:2, 4–6)

Recalling the past was a Hebraic thing to do. Throughout their history they understood who God was by what he had done. They viewed life differently to us; our view is that the past is the past and we face the future. The Jews, however, believed that the future was in God's hands. They faced the future by looking behind. This is like our riding on a train with our back to the engine. We are going forward, but as we go, we are constantly seeing the past.

As they looked back, they were specifically to remember the sins of their ancestors, the consequences of that sin, and how ultimately they were brought to the place of acknowledging that the Lord had been right all the time.

The very people engaged in the work of restoration were clearly in danger of making the same mistakes as their forefathers. No specific sins are mentioned, but that they were not living lives appropriate to the covenant people of God is apparent. They were in danger of history repeating itself.

What lessons can we learn by remembering the past? Memory can often be the first step on the way back. Jonah, from inside the fish, engaged in this process of remembering and it led to a change of mind (Jonah 2).

In the far country, the prodigal son suddenly remembered his father and decided to return (Luke 15:17).

Return to the Lord (1:3)

This is what the LORD Almighty says: 'Return to me,' declares the LORD Almighty, 'and I will return to you.'

This is the heart of the matter. God's people must always live in a state of repentance. Zechariah was doing what the prophets before him and since have always done; calling God's people back to the covenant relationship. Only as we are rightly related to the Lord, do we find that life is really worth living.

When something goes wrong there is a choice to be made. We

may choose to be resentful and blame someone or anyone else for the mess that we are in. We may decide that happiness is to be found in the world and try to find satisfaction in the pursuit of pleasure. The Lord says there is another choice, *'Return to me'*. Now repentance is agreeing with God about everything. The hardest thing about repentance is the acceptance that we were wrong. But 'Godly sorrow brings repentance that leads to salvation and leaves no regret' (2 Corinthians 7:10). Genuine repentance has no regrets. It is a change of mind which leads to a change of life. There is a healing, purifying operation in repentance.

As we make that first step we have the promise, 'And I will return to you.' In response to our coming, the free unmerited favour of God comes to us, cancels our debts, imputes and imparts Christ's righteousness to us. The broken relationship is restored – Hallelujah!

Haggai and Zechariah used different methods to motivate God's people, but they are agreed about this, it is not enough to serve God, it must be accompanied by a fundamental change of heart, so that what we do will ensure that it is God's will, done in his way. This is the challenge to the church of Jesus Christ today.

Questions

1. What lessons can we learn by remembering the past? Each person share.
2. What do you understand by repentance? What place is there for corporate repentance. i.e., is there something for which your local church needs to repent?
3. Can a nation repent? Recent examples include Germany (the holocaust), Japan (treatment of prisoners of war). Perhaps Britain should repent for its past treatment of Ireland (17th century massacres, 19th century famines). Are words enough to satisfy the aggrieved? Does restitution make sense?

4

A SERIES OF
EIGHT VISIONS

Zechariah 1:7 – 6:8

Zechariah 1:7–17

The man among the myrtle trees

The man among the myrtle trees is the leader of God's messengers sent throughout the earth. They return with a message of encouragement.

Zechariah not only preached straightforward messages, but also communicated truth through the more mystical vision. In fact, the major part of the first section of his book is taken up with a series of eight visions that he experienced in just one night (1:7 – 6:15).

That God spoke and speaks through visions should not surprise us. He is a supernatural God who employs supernatural means (see *Visions*, p. 57). The vision belongs to the prophetic tradition of both Old and New Testament (Amos 7–9; Acts 10:9–16; 11:4–18).

What the prophet saw (1:8)

He saw a valley with myrtle trees. Standing amongst the trees there was a man riding a red horse. Behind him were other horses, coloured red, brown and white. The similarity of these visions with those of the book of Revelation are striking.

The myrtle tree, for instance, symbolizes Israel in its restoration (Isaiah 55:13). The myrtle tree has fragrant flowers and spicy sweet centred leaves. All parts of the tree are perfumed. Isaiah used the picture to contrast Israel's thorny, briar-like chastening experience to its restoration as a fragrant myrtle tree.

Now Israel was being restored, but was still in a valley – not yet through it – but being reminded that they were not alone.

There was a man riding a red horse amongst them. Surely the man was a pre-incarnate appearance of our Lord Jesus Christ, the same man that Joshua saw standing between him and Jericho, with a drawn sword in his hand. There the man was described as the commander of the Lord's armies (Joshua 5:13–14). Here he is riding a red horse, either naturally red or dyed red with the blood of war as the champion of God appeared in Isaiah's vision (Isaiah 63:1–2). Red is also the colour of fire, perhaps pointing the reader to God's anger against the nations who went beyond their mandate to chasten Israel and 'added to the calamity' (Zechariah 1:15).

John's revelation of God's 'Conqueror bent on conquest' riding a white horse (Revelation 6:2; 19:11), reveals that he has now fought the battle, gained the victory and rides in triumph.

What the prophet heard (1:9–17)

This is where the angel enters the vision, talking to Zechariah and offering to provide understanding for the vision (1:9). It is the man on the red horse who speaks and informs the prophet that he has been leading a reconnaissance party throughout the earth. He reports that the whole world is 'at rest and in peace' (1:11).

This report that all was seemingly well in the world was not apparently good news and provokes intercession by the mediator (1:12), asking God to intervene in the world's affairs on Judah's behalf.

To understand the reason behind this prayer see Haggai 2:22, 'I will overturn royal thrones and shatter the power of the foreign kingdoms. I will overthrow chariots and their drivers;

horses and their riders will fall, each by the sword of his brother.' The citizens of Jerusalem were expecting God to intervene dramatically and destroy the foreign kingdoms.

Peace in the world was therefore a problem they could not understand. They had served their seventy years' sentence and now the angel of the LORD asks God on their behalf to end the dominion that their enemies still exercised over them (cf. verse 12 and Jeremiah 25:11). What a lovely picture this is of Christ interceding for his church (see Hebrews 7:25).

Zechariah also heard the Lord's kind and comforting words (1:13). It was a reminder that 'God was still on the throne and he will remember his own.' They were not to understand from the present, peaceful scene that all was well with the nations of the world. Nor should peace be a comfort to those who think that they have got away with murder. Our God reigns and justice will be done.

What the prophet had to do (1:14, 17)

He had to continue to preach the word. For Zechariah it was a twofold message – he had to proclaim the wrath of God on his enemies and the mercy of God towards his people.

Proclaim the wrath of God on his enemies (1:14–15)

The reason that God was to reveal his anger to the nations is stated as being that they 'added to the calamity', that is, they went beyond the limits which God allowed in chastening his people. These nations are now at rest and peace, which they do not deserve, but they are shortly to be disturbed.

Proclaim the mercy of God to his people (1:16–17)

God's mercy would be seen in the divinely inspired rebuilding of the temple, and the rehabitation of the ruined city. God's people had a hope and a future despite the appearance to the contrary. Let's not forget Jerusalem was still in a sorry state, its walls ruined and its great buildings in disrepair. The work on the restoration of the temple had only just started. It could not have been easy to believe that God was blessing his chosen people, under such circumstances.

There are times in our own experience when our circumstances challenge us to question the love and the mercy of God. There are times when everything seems to be against us including God himself. At such times we need to listen to the Word of God.

Questions

1. What do you think this vision would have said most clearly to the citizens of Jerusalem and what does it have to say to us today?
2. What place, if any, do visions have in the Church of Jesus Christ today?
3. What message do we have to proclaim prophetically now to the nations of the world? How can it be done so that they will fear?

Visions

That God spoke through visions in the Old and New Testament is undeniable. The question I suggest might be discussed by groups and thought through by individuals is, 'What place, if any, do visions have in the Church of Jesus Christ today?'

There is a big debate going on in the church about this matter. All evangelical Christians would agree that God's Word is complete and no truth can be added to holy Scripture. Some evangelicals want to say more, adding that none of the prophetic revelatory gifts have a place in the worship and ministry of the church today. They argue that God revealed his

Word in Old Testament times until the final writings of Ezra and Nehemiah. There followed 400 'silent' years, when no prophet spoke God's revelation. That silence was broken by John the Baptist as God spoke once more prior to the New Testament age. God then gave New Testament revelation which ceased with the writings of the Apostle John. By the second century AD the canon (the books which make up the Bible) was popularly recognized. Finalization and closing of the canon occurred in the fourth century. This is very important because it is comparable to the Old Testament canon that closed and was followed by silence. God's pattern for the New Testament seems to have been the same – revelatory silence after the closing of the canon.

Certainly there are dangers associated with being open to mystical visions. In the history of the church many have been misled by them and there are some very notable cases in point. The answer to abuse of a gift, however, is not non-use but right use. There is ample biblical and historical evidence to support that God still speaks through dreams and visions.

Peter, on the day of Pentecost, explained the phenomenon that they all witnessed by quoting from the prophet Joel: 'In the last days, God says, I will pour out my Spirit on all people. Your sons and daughters will prophesy, your young men will see visions, your old men will dream dreams. Even on my servants, both men and women, I will pour out my Spirit in those days, and they will prophesy' (Acts 2:17–18). The day of Pentecost historically was the day when the Spirit was initially poured upon all flesh.

It is interesting to note that whenever Revival fires have fallen on the church it has seen the re-emergence of the supernatural, extra-biblical revelations.

Therefore visions must always be tested The Bible warns against false prophets, false dreams and false visions (Jeremiah 14:14; Ezekiel 13:3–7; Zechariah 10:2). Visions may be from God, but they may be the result of a creative mind or a crafty devil! How can we know if they are from the Lord? I would suggest four safeguards:

1. It must not in any way contradict Scripture, but must be consistent with sound doctrine and established Christian principles.

2. It must glorify God; so ask who is exalted by the vision. The giver or the receiver? The Apostle Paul knew the dangers of boasting about visions (2 Corinthians 12:7).

3. It must have confirmation. Either the vision wlll confirm something that Scripture has already said, or some subsequent event should confirm the vision. When the Angel Gabriel appeared to Mary in a vision, he gave her clear signs so that she would know he was from God (Luke 1:26–38).

4. It should be submitted to those who are over us in the Lord for testing. All the gifts and manifestations of the Holy Spirit belong to the body of Christ (1 Corinthians 12:4–11) and understanding and interpreting visions belong to the local church (1 Corinthians 14:32).

The Lord has no new truth to add to that revealed in Scripture, but will sometimes use visions and other means of communication to reveal some truth about ourselves or others that will help us in our ministry for him. As Christians we need to 'walk in the Spirit' and develop a sensitivity to the ways in which God might apply biblical truths to us, but we also need to exercise proper safeguards so as to protect believers from deception or exploitation.

Zechariah 1:18-21

The four horns

The people of God can expect opposition from all quarters, but if we ask him the Lord will show us how he intends to deal with it.

God's people are at war, but the battle is the Lord's and the victory has already been secured. The second vision of the night serves to illustrate this truth.

The four horns (1:18-19)

> Then I looked up – and there before me were four horns! I asked the angel who was speaking to me, 'What are these?'
>
> He answered me, 'These are the horns that scattered Judah, Israel and Jerusalem.'(1:18-19)

In Scripture the horn is always the symbol of strength and power. The four horns speak of the four quarters of the earth, not just international aggression, but opposition from wherever it comes. The horns 'that *scattered* Judah, Israel and Jerusalem': the word 'scattered' need not necessarily refer to being taken into captivity but can mean 'endeavoured to destroy national unity'.

The Jews could not forget that they were the chosen people of God. To them, that involved the certainty that some day they would arrive at world supremacy. In their early history they looked forward to the coming of someone of King David's line who would unite the nation and lead them to greatness (Isaiah 11:1). God would raise up a righteous branch for David (Jeremiah 23:5). Some day the people would serve David their king (Jeremiah 30:9). David would be their shepherd and their king (Ezekiel 34:23; 37:24). And out of Bethlehem there would come a ruler who would be great to the ends of the earth (Micah 5:2–4).

But the whole history of Israel seemed to deny these hopes. After the death of Solomon, the kingdom, small enough to begin with, split into two under their kings Rehoboam and Jeroboam and so lost its unity. The Northern kingdom, with its capital at Samaria, vanished in the last quarter of the 8th century BC overrun by the Assyrians and never to be seen again in history. The Southern kingdom, with its capital at Jerusalem, was reduced to slavery and exile by the Babylonians, which brings us up to the point in Israel's history that we are dealing with now. History for the Jews was a catalogue of disasters from which it became clear that no human Deborah could rescue them (see Judges 4:4–16).

These horns represent all those forces who sought to impoverish them. Some commentators have tried to identify the four horns as particular international powers, but I believe it wiser to see them as a picture of the enemies of the church from wherever they come. In all these visions we have to ask ourselves this question, 'What would it have meant to those to whom this revelation was first given?' If you read through Ezra chapter four and Nehemiah chapter four, you can identify some of the 'enemies of Judah and Benjamin'. I have no doubt, reading those chapters, whom the citizens of Jerusalem would have seen as these bull-like horns.

The Apostle Paul, I believe, was addressing the same problem when he wrote, 'Finally, be strong in the Lord and in his mighty power. Put on the full armour of God so that you can take your stand against the devil's schemes. For our struggle is not against flesh and blood . . .' (Ephesians 6:10–12). Spiritual warfare is not just a human struggle, supernatural forces are ranged against us. In similar apocalyptic style the great enemy of the New Testament church is described by John as having seven heads and ten horns (Revelation 17:3). Whenever we declare ourselves to be on the Lord's side and we identify ourselves with his work we can expect to be attacked. The old arch enemy of God's people still wants to divide and conquer.

The four craftsmen (1:20–21)

The four craftsmen are revealed as those that the Lord has sent 'to terrify . . . and throw down' the enemies of God's people. Just as the people of Judah had been so terrified that they couldn't lift their heads to look at them, so now the time has come for the tables to be turned. Just as a dangerous bull might have to have its horns removed to make it harmless, so too the opponents of God's people would be disarmed by God's servants.

There were four horns and so the Lord raises up four craftsmen. There are some ingenious suggestions as to whom the craftsmen were, but they don't have to be identified. However, I do like the idea that they might have been Ezra, Nehemiah, Zerubbabel and Joshua. They fit the role well, but it simply doesn't matter. What is true is that when God has a work to do, he will raise up people to do it and others to defend and protect them while they are engaged in doing it.

God always acts on behalf of his children. Christians have all they need in Jesus Christ. He has all authority (Matthew 28:18). He promises us power to stand for him (Acts 1:8). 'If God is for us, who can be against us?' (Romans 8:31–39).

We cannot overcome the 'horns' that oppose us, but Jesus already has. We are at war, but the victory has already been won. Let us keep our eyes on Jesus 'the author and perfecter of our faith,' depending on his mighty power 'for no weapon forged against you will prevail' (Hebrews 12:2 and Isaiah 54:17).

Questions

1. When trials or temptations come, what help can we expect from Jesus Christ? Find and discuss some examples.
2. The devil's strategy with the church has always been to divide and conquer. What are the greatest threats to divide your church and what is the answer to it?
3. Share what you find to be the secret to victorious Christian living?

Apocalyptic writing

Haggai and Zechariah were, as we have seen already, contemporaries. Both were prophets but their style was different. Haggai was clearly an inspired preacher. Zechariah, however, went beyond Haggai and he has been rightly called the apocalyptic writer of the Old Testament. The difference between the prophets and the apocalyptists was very real. Haggai and Zechariah had the same message, they were both determined to encourage the people to carry on the work of rebuilding the temple. Their methods, however, were different. The prophets' message was invariably spoken, whereas the message of the apocalyptist was always written. Apocalyptic is a literary production. Had it been delivered by word of mouth people would never have understood it. It is difficult and has to be carefully and prayerfully considered.

All apocalyptic literature deals with these events, the sin of the present age, the terrors of the time between and the blessings of the time to come. It is entirely composed of dreams and visions of the end. It is continually attempting to describe the indescribable.

This is further complicated by another fact. It was only natural that these apocalyptic visions should really appeal to those living under tyranny and oppression. The more foreign powers held them down, the more they dreamt of the destruction of that power and of their own relief. It would only have inflamed the situation, however, if the oppressing power could have understood those visions and dreams, so the powers are not named and the visions are quoted in language which was not distinguishable to the outsider. Therefore, the more we know about the historical background, the better we can interpret the visions.

Apocalypse means revelation. It is another means that God has employed to reveal himself and his purposes to his people.

Zechariah 2:1–13

The unwanted tape-measure

Jerusalem is not to be measured. There is room for everyone in the Lord's city.

In this chapter the actual vision is recorded in the first five verses. The rest of the chapter (2:6–13) is taken up with the prophet illustrating and expanding the meaning of the  revelation. As you read verses 6–13 you may sense that the words have a different flow and feel about them. Verses 6–9 and verses 10–13 are two stanzas of a poem. It had been written especially for those who were still in Babylon, or even for the descendants of those scattered from the fall of Israel over 200 years earlier. The vision with the poem is a call to return to Jerusalem.

It is estimated that at the time of Zechariah's visions of the night some forty thousand people had already returned to Jerusalem, but there were even more still living in Babylon. As an old commentator put it, 'The land of their captivity had become the land of their nativity'. Babylon was the only home most of these people now knew and many, like Nehemiah, had good jobs and comfortable lives (Nehemiah 2:1). Nevertheless they were to be stirred and motivated to come home.

Rebuilding the city

This third vision is linked to the first and continues to develop the same truth: 'The measuring line will be stretched out over Jerusalem ' (1:16). The whole of the city is to be rebuilt. God the King has chosen Jerusalem (1:17; 2:12) and in addition wants to bless the inhabitants.

Thus the city was in the process of reconstruction, but was largely still a mountain of rubble. The young man with the measuring line is going to survey the city, but is prevented from doing so by an angel who, in figurative language, tells him that Jerusalem will grow so much that it will be impossible for it to have walls. Like all the great cities of the world it was to know urban sprawl. The Lord's presence will be so glorious that he himself will be as a wall to it. Now that was tremendously encouraging to Zechariah's congregation. It was also an encouragement for other exiles to return home. Clearly it wasn't to be understood literally because ultimately the Lord raised up Nehemiah to get the walls built. The whole point was that Jehovah would cause the city to grow, would guard them, and fill the city with his glory.

Building the church

Zechariah however, has an even bigger vision than most. He sees the day when the covenant with Jehovah will be opened to many nations (2:11), predicting no doubt the addition of Gentile nations to form the church of the Messiah. That this and other Old Testament prophecies speak to us of the formation of the New Testament church there can be no doubt. Not only does the New Testament remind us that 'All Scripture is God-breathed and is useful for teaching ... ' (2 Timothy 3:16), but more specifically it assures Christian people that 'We have come to Mount Zion . . . ' (Hebrews 12:22).

From the Christian perspective, the prophet's anticipation of Gentiles joining the flood for the holy city is given substance in the birth and growth of the Christian church.

This message then, is to all God's people and should be applied to us in the new covenant. The church is as the city – impossible to measure. There are no definable boundaries. We might therefore learn:

1. The church is to be a growing church

Compare 2:4 and 11. Throughout the history of the church there have been those that have attempted to restrict it to certain boundaries. Compare Acts 10:35 and Galatians 3:28.

2. The church is to be a guarded church

Compare 2:5, 8–9; Psalms 7:10; 31:2; 59:9; 62:2 and 89:18. This ancient description of how God perceived the nation of Israel as the apple of his eye has sometimes been difficult to understand. At some points in the history of the Jewish nation this has been called into question. Bitter power struggles, ongoing tensions in the Middle East and smouldering ancient rivalries have kept the descendants of Abraham, Isaac and Jacob in either an orphaned or a vulnerable position. Without a home, for many centuries the Jews have been maligned, persecuted and scattered throughout the earth. In fact so fierce has been the opposition and so vicious have been the attacks upon them as a people that millions of Jews have been slaughtered throughout the ages.

Similarly in the history of the church of Jesus Christ it has been a continual story of opposition and persecution.

3. The church is to be a glorious church

Compare 2:5 and 11–12. It is the Lord's presence himself that makes the church attractive. This prophecy received a glorious fulfilment in the great event recorded by John, 'The Word became flesh and made his dwelling amongst us. We have seen his glory, the glory of the One and Only, who came from the Father, full of grace and truth' (John 1:1). The truth is that this same Jesus who came to Bethlehem, who was crucified, buried and rose again is still alive and present in his church.

Zechariah chapter 2 closes in a strange way. The prophet calls everyone to be still, because this big powerful being is stirring himself and is at work on behalf of his people (2:13).

Questions

1. What evidence would you produce to prove God's protection of you?
2. Some Christians prefer small churches; but should every church be a growing church?
3. What makes the church different from any other organization? Compare it with your government, for instance, the United Nations, the Red Cross and any local organisations that you can think of.

Zion

The prophet sometimes refers to Jerusalem as Zion. In the Old Testament Zion is one of the hills on which Jerusalem stood. It is first mentioned in 2 Samuel 5:7, 'David captured the fortress of Zion, the city of David'. At this time the citadel probably stood at the long ridge running south of the temple, although not all scholars are agreed on this. This location is near the only known spring; it is suitable for defence; its size is about that of other fortified towns; archaeological remains show that it was inhabited long before David's time and certain Bible references (1 Kings 8:1; 2 Chronicles 5:2; 32:30; 33:14) indicate that this was the original Zion. David brought the ark to Zion and the hill then became sacred (2 Samuel 6:10–12). When Solomon later removed the ark to the temple the name Zion was extended to take in the temple (Isaiah 8:18; 18:7; 24:23; Joel 3:17; Micah 4:7). Zion came to be used for the whole of Jerusalem (2 Kings 19:21; Psalms 48; 69:35; 133:3; Isaiah 1:8; *etc.*).

When we come to the New Testament, however, Zion is no longer described in the ethnic, territorial and economic way which the Old Testament uses. Instead of a physical temple and city to make visible the reality of God's kingdom we have a new and living way (compare John 4:22ff and Hebrews 10:19–21), even Jesus himself. By entering the new covenant Christian believers have already joined heavenly worshippers and 'have come to Mount Zion, to the heaven Jerusalem, the city of the living God.' (Hebrews 12:22, compare Revelation 14:1). There is no sacred city, shrine or site on earth which gives access to God's presence as did the Old Testament Zion.

It is true that Paul foresees the day when '. . . all Israel will be saved, as it is written: "The deliverer will come from Zion"' (Romans 11:26–27). The salvation referred to in this passage may well take place in that day when the Messiah reigns upon the earth in righteousness and peace.

That the nation of Israel was very special in the sight of God is undeniable. To it were given promises, a covenant, a land and many other blessings, all of this because of God's purposes for it. Even though the nation has failed God, he remains faithful to his word. God will accomplish his purposes through Israel. Notwithstanding all this, the same Apostle Paul wrote, 'You are all sons of God through faith in Christ Jesus, for all of you who were baptised into Christ have clothed yourselves with Christ. There is neither Jew nor Greek, slave nor free, male nor female, for you are all one in Christ Jesus. If you belong to Christ, then you are Abraham's seed and heirs according to the promise' (Galatians 3:26–29). Until Christ returns, in this age of the Christian church, we must understand Zion as a picture of the church and citizenship of it is open only as we become children of God through faith in Christ Jesus.

Apple of the eye

'For whoever touches you, touches the apple of his eye' (2:8). The apple of the eye is understood as the eyeball or the pupil in its centre, protected by the eyelids automatically closing when anything approaches too near. It is a symbol of that which is precious and protected (see Deuteronomy 32:10; Psalm 17:8; Proverbs 7:2).

Zechariah 3:1–10

Clean clothes

The Lord has provided adequate defence for every accusation brought against his children.

In this fourth vision the prophet saw Joshua, the high priest, standing before the angel of the Lord, but clothed in filthy garments. On his right hand Satan stood as his accuser, but the Lord spoke up for him and also provided him with clean clothes and new headgear. He was then recommissioned as a guardian of the moral and spiritual life of God's people (3:1–7).

Remember that this is still a vision of the night (1:8), but the subject of this vision is a real character, Zechariah's own colleague Joshua, who was the actual high priest in Jerusalem (3:1). However, Joshua here represents the whole people of God in the old and the new covenants. 'Listen, O high priest Joshua and your associates seated before you, who are men *symbolic of things to come*' (3:8: author's italics).

The access that we have to the Lord (3:1)

'Then he showed me Joshua the high priest standing before the angel of the LORD, and Satan standing at his right side to accuse him. The LORD said . . .' (3:1). The scene depicted is like that of a court. God is acting in the role of the judge, with Satan at his hand in the role of accuser, or prosecuting attorney. Notice that Joshua was standing before the Lord. It prompts these questions: What is our standing with God? Have we come to him through the access that is made (compare John 14:6 and Hebrews 10:19–22)?

The accuser that we have (3:2)

'Satan standing at his right side to accuse him' (3:2). Satan in Hebrew means the 'opposer' or 'accuser'. This is not the only place in the Bible where he is described in this way (see Job 1:6–12 and Revelation 12:10). Accusation is his business day and night before the throne of God. And if he has courage to do that before God, imagine what he is capable of doing to us, even though he knows that we have access to the Lord and are known personally by him. Satan tells us all manner of lies (see 2 Timothy 2:26; 1 Peter 5:8, 9). Satan's real success with his accusations is that he sows seeds of doubt that, if we listen they become a foothold from which he builds a stronghold (compare Ephesians 4:27 with 2 Corinthians 10:4, 5).

The advocate we have (3:2)

The Lord is judge, but as soon as the prosecuting counsel makes his case, the judge steps in and becomes the advocate for the accused. The judge is our friend – hallelujah! This is really good news, because if the judge is on our side there can be no doubt as to the outcome of the case.

The advocate was dealing with Satan personally, and tells him that his accusation is doomed to fail for two reasons: Firstly, 'The LORD who has chosen Jerusalem, rebuke you!' is saying, don't you realize that when I called these people, I knew all their failings (Romans 8:29). It might be saying in effect, that if he knew about their sins when he chose them to be part of his covenant people, he is certainly not going to reject them because of the same sins now.

Secondly, 'Is not this man a burning stick snatched from the fire?' Joshua and all these people in Jerusalem were just this. They have just been rescued from the fires of oppression in Babylon. God is saying in effect that his purpose is to set his people free, not to bring them back into bondage. Thank God that every converted person 'is a burning stick snatched from the fire' and this by a miracle of God's grace. Therefore we will never be left to the devices of Satan.

The admission that we have to make (3:3–5)

Compare 3:3–5 and Romans 3:23–24. When we confess the contamination and filthiness of our sins, God delights to take all away and transfer his righteousness to us.

The authority we must accept (3:6–7)

What a turnabout here. The Joshua that was on trial at thre at of his job, is now being reaffirmed and recommissioned to the task to which he is called. If Joshua or any one of us, is to exercise authority in the church of Jesus Christ, we have first of

71

all to be under the Lord's authority. We have to walk in his ways and keep his requirements if we are to fulfil our calling (see Matthew 8:5–13). You can be sure that if there is an area of your life where you are not experiencing victory, then there will be an area of your life not under the authority of our Lord Jesus Christ.

The announcement that was made (3:8–10)

In the remaining verses we have a clear prophecy of the coming Messiah. All that Joshua and his associates represented were symbols, or types, of the Messiah to come. Here is a reaffirmation of God's purpose to install on a Judean throne 'The Branch' (3:8), a king from David's line (see Jeremiah 23:5).

The engraved stone referred to in verses 8–9 symbolizes the stone in the High Priest's ephod (compare Exodus 28:9ff). The removal of sin in a single day was fulfilled on the cross (see John 1:29).

The message ends on this note of forgiveness, reverting to the theme of the vision. The people of God are promised security and peace. The accuser has been silenced, the offence has been dealt with, there is nothing to hinder reconciliation and rejoicing taking place.

Questions

1. How real is the activity of Satan and how does he make accusations?
2. What do you understand by 'imputed' righteousness? In Christ God regards us as if we had not sinned (see Romans 8:1–14). How does this help us to live better lives?
3. What moral and spiritual responsibilities are placed upon God's people in the teaching of this chapter?

'In that day' (3:10)

We have come across this phrase before (see *The day of the LORD* p. 46), and it is a familiar futuristic phrase in the Old Testament. It looks forward to the day of the Messiah, when God's people will live together in extraordinary contentment, sharing together the blessings of an age of peace. There is little doubt that many of the people thought this day would coincide with the completion and consecration of the temple. It wasn't, nor did it find its complete fulfilment at the first coming of our Lord Jesus Christ.

'Each of you will invite his neighbour to sit under his vine and fig tree' (3:10) is reminiscent of 1 Kings 4:25, Micah 4:4 and others. It is an announcement of the approaching fulfilment of the promise of Jeremiah, 'In those days and at that time I will make a righteous Branch sprout from David's line; he will do what is just and right in the land. In those days Judah will be saved and Jerusalem will live in safety. This is the day by which it will be called: "The LORD Our Righteousness"' (Jeremiah 33:15–16).

Such prophecies were partially fulfilled in the restoration of the Jews after the captivity and further fulfilled at the first coming of Jesus, but their complete fulfilment is to be expected in the future when, ' . . . all Israel will be saved, as it is written' (Romans 11:26). Since no Bible prophecy has ever failed, isn't it reasonable to accept with confidence its predictions that are still unfulfilled? They were given by the same God. They have equal authority and they will come to pass. When Christ comes again all the prophecies concerning his righteous rule will be fulfilled in every detail. Lasting peace will prevail. Righteousness will reign. Poverty will be abolished and harmony between individuals and nations will be established.

73

Zechariah 4:1–14

Apparatus for anointing

**The Lord's work is never easy, but it is his work
and he is always on hand to help us with it.**

It isn't easy being a Christian. Whether you belong to a small fellowship or a large one there are times when it appears that we are not making much headway. Perhaps we  can't find sufficient volunteers for the work, there is opposition from outside and disharmony inside, or perhaps it is the cash flow that is hindering progress, or perhaps you have members who remember how great the church used to be – before you joined it. It can all be so discouraging!

This is exactly how the citizens of Jerusalem were feeling (Haggai 2:3). To these people the Lord speaks through the fifth vision of the night. Two phrases from this chapter have been used as often as any other scripture to encourage and challenge God's people: '"Not by might, nor by power, but by my Spirit", says the LORD Almighty' (4:6) and 'Who despises the day of small things?' (4:10).

The golden lampstand

Zechariah appears to be nodding off in the middle of all these visions and needed to be nudged awake by the angel of the Lord. He is not the first to have fallen asleep during inspired revelations. Like all good communicators, the angel asked a question of Zechariah to keep his attention, 'What do you see?' He then begins to see again. 'I see a solid gold lampstand with a bowl at the top and seven lights on it, with seven channels to the lights. Also there are two olive trees by it, one on the right of the bowl and the other on its left' (4:2–3).

Visualize this oil lamp at the top of the pedestal. The lamp contains a bowl filled with oil. Seven wicks protruding from the bowl are individual burners. The fuel of the lamp is olive oil, which is piped directly from the two olive trees, either side of the pedestal (4:2–3). It undoubtedly refers to the light that never goes out in the temple (compare Exodus 30:7–8 with 2 Chronicles 29:7). As such it speaks of the restoration of full worship when the temple has been rebuilt.

The two leaders, Joshua the high priest featured in the last vision and Zerubbabel the governor, are finding the going tough, a 'mighty mountain' (4:7) of difficulties hinder the work, but it is going to be levelled and through this anointed leadership the work will be completed. The temple capstone, when put in place, will be met with the hallelujah chorus (4:7). A distinct word to Zechariah spells out what it meant (4:9); Zerubbabel will complete the work as a validation of his prophetic ministry.

The building of the temple took five years from 520 to 515 BC (Ezra 6:15) and there were times when they thought they would never get there, but the day was coming when the governor would hold up the plumb-line for the last time (4:10).

Explanation of the details of the vision follow: the seven lights are 'The eyes of the LORD which range throughout the earth'. It might speak of the all-seeing presence of God, but it also speaks surely of God's people as lights in the darkness (compare with Revelation 1:12–20). They are supported and fed by the olive trees which, to the original hearers of the vision, would have spoken of Joshua and Zerubbabel. Though reference to Ezra 6:14

shows that the prophets Haggai and Zechariah would also have fitted this description.

What abiding lessons from this vision speak to us today?

1. God's purposes must be fulfilled (4:6)

'"Not by might, nor by power, but by my Spirit", says the LORD Almighty.' Might and power were both used in the work of restoration and are still appropriate to be used in the work of the kingdom. However, it is the Spirit of God that brings success. All manpower, provisions of materials and expertise are part of the Lord's plan, but his Spirit must unify all that is done to fulfil his purposes and verse 7 reminds us that it is all by God's grace.

2. God's people are the channels through which he works (4:9)

Both the governor Zerubbabel and the prophet Zechariah are referred to here and serve to remind us of the important part that people play in the work of God's kingdom. The golden lampstand stood in the Holy Place as the symbol of God's peoples' true position as light in the darkness (compare Isaiah 60:3; Matthew 5:14, 16).

The church depends for its effective witness upon every member finding their place in the body of Christ. Through all the members of the Christian church the life and light of God must be made available to the world.

3. God's power is always available to help us in the task

Throughout Scripture, oil is the symbol of the Holy Spirit. It was used for anointing kings, priests and prophets (see 1 Samuel 10:1; Leviticus 8:30; Isaiah 61:1). In the parable of the ten virgins we see the importance of having oil in our lamps. Without oil there is no life, and without life there is no light. The apostle writes, 'Anyone who does not have the Spirit of Christ does not belong to Christ' (Romans 8:9). This is exactly how we are to understand the work of the Spirit in this vision (compare 4:6

and 11–14). No-one can expect to have a great deal of success in carrying out the purposes of God and in being lights in this dark world until they have been filled with the life-giving power that makes effective witness possible (Acts 1:8).

Questions

1. What experience have you had that made you aware of God's Holy Spirit in your life? Each share.
2. How does your church help people discover, develop and use their gifts?
3. When do you think it appropriate, if ever, to use the world's 'might and power' to further God's kingdom?

Plumb-line (4:10)

A plumb-line is a cord with a stone or metal weight, the plummet, tied to one end; it is used in testing whether a wall is perpendicular and on this occasion can be understood literally. Plumb-line and plummet are used figuratively of God's action in testing the uprightness of his people on many occasions in the Scriptures (Amos 7:7–9; 2 Kings 21:31; Isaiah 28:17).

Zechariah 5:1–4

The flying scroll

**Renewal is always accompanied by the exposing
of sin which must be dealt with in God's way.**

The message of the two visions in Zechariah
chapter five is that God requires moral purity
amongst his people. The curse on sin is
emphasized and the call for sanctification is
expressed in a call for commitment to the revealed moral will of
God. Two particular sins are dealt with in the first vision; theft
and bearing false witness in the Lord's name.

God's curse

Imagine a light aircraft with a banner trailing from it making an
announcement and you have the picture of the flying scroll.
There are two messages, one on either side of the banner which
is thirty feet long and fifteen feet wide. It serves as God's curse
or sentence on sin. The sins specified are theft and swearing
falsely in God's name. The sentence announced on both sides of
the banner is the same, banishment and destruction of his home.
Presumably the third and the eighth of the ten commandments
are referred to as an example of sin against the Lord and our
neighbours.

Don't miss what the Lord Almighty adds to the vision, 'I will send it out and it will enter the house of the thief and the house of him who swears falsely by my name. It will remain in his house and destroy it, both its timbers and its stones' (5:4). The Lord is seen here as a missile that is to be personally delivered into every person's home.

Now observe the movement of these visions of the night. They have dealt with the temple and the leaders of the people, but now they focus on making known the requirements of the law throughout the whole land.

Yes, the building needed restoring, the priests have to be holy, all the leaders need to be anointed, but the purpose is to restore the nation into its covenant relationship with God. To this end the law is to be proclaimed throughout the land. The apostle Paul dealt with this very issue in Romans chapter 3. In contrasting God's faithfulness with the sinfulness of people everywhere, he explains the place of the law, 'Now we know that whatever the law says, it says to those who are under the law, so that every mouth may be silenced and the whole world held accountable to God. Therefore no-one will be declared righteous in his sight by observing the law, rather, through the law we become conscious of sin' (Romans 3:19–20).

God's people are to stand as priests interceding (3:1–10) and as the light illuminating (4:1–14), but God's people in this vision are called upon to apply the principles of the law throughout the land.

God's good news

John had a similar vision of a flying scroll recorded for us in Revelation 14:6, 'I saw another angel flying in mid-air and he had the eternal gospel to proclaim to those who live on the earth – to every nation, tribe, language and people.' This angel comes with the eternal gospel. The gospel is eternally valid; even in a world which is crashing to its doom, its truth still stands. It also means of course, the gospel that has existed from all eternity.

Not insignificantly this angel is followed by another who said, 'Fallen! Fallen is Babylon the Great, which made all the nations drink the maddening wine of her adulteries' (Revelation 14:6–8). It is significant that the angel with the gospel is followed immediately by the angels of doom. The gospel has of necessity a double-edged quality. It is good news for those who receive it, but it is judgment to those who reject it. And the condemnation of those who reject it is all the greater because they were given the chance to accept it.

The challenge to us is, how are we going to make the good news, and the bad news known? The Lord Almighty declares, 'I will send it out, and it will enter the house of the thief and the house of him who swears falsely by my name' (Zechariah 5:4). The Lord has sent it out. The church of Jesus Christ is under orders to go (Matthew 28:19).

The young man dressed up as a clown and walked through the streets carrying two placards. The one in front of him read, 'I'm a fool for Christ's sake'. The one behind him read, 'Who's fool are you?' He was at least ingenious in his method of evangelism! He had entrance into places where many of us could never get. Where there's a will, there's a way. Inspiration leads to ingenuity. These visions of the night challenge us at this very point.

Questions

1. What does this vision reveal about the moral conditions that are required to accompany any renewing work of God? Compare 2 Timothy 2:19.
2. What significance do you see in the fact that the sins specified are stealing and swearing falsely by the Lord's name?
3. What effects would these two sins have in any society, and particularly in one recovering from financial depression and political upheaval?

The flying scroll

The dimensions of the flying scroll, are 'Thirty feet long and fifteen feet wide' (5:2). These dimensions correspond to those of the holy place of the tabernacle and also of the porch of Solomon's temple. If we were to consider the measurement of the scroll as symbolic, we may regard it as indicating that the measure of the sanctuary is the measure of sin: that is to say, the sinner must not say, 'I am not worse than my neighbour', but should measure his conduct by the Lord's higher standard. Jesus said, 'Be perfect, therefore, as your heavenly father is perfect.'

Zechariah 5:5–11

The woman in a basket

Wickedness has no place amongst God's people.

You could well be thinking that you are now in the middle of a pantomime, for the imagery is bizarre. This vision is in two parts. Firstly, there is a measuring basket or barrel which is identified as 'the iniquity of the people throughout the land' (5:6). The 'measuring basket' was a large container by which, in earlier times measures were estimated. The explanation given (5:6) indicates that God's people had been 'weighed on scales' and found wanting (compare Daniel 5:27).

81

The Lord clearly had the measure of the nation's immoral condition.

This basket had a lead cover, which was lifted to reveal a woman who is wickedness personified. As soon as she is exposed she is covered up again. Then two other women enter the picture. They have wings like those of a stork and they are flying. They lifted up the basket and took it to 'The country of Babylonia to build a house for it. When it is ready the basket will be set there in its place' (5:11). The message is plain, there is no place for any wickedness amongst God's people.

The reference to Babylonia is significant, as it was the place from which these people had so recently returned from seventy years of captivity. It was the place of chastening. In the vision of the flying scrolls, specific sins are mentioned, whereas in this vision it is 'wickedness' that is exposed. A *woman* is used in the vision because the Hebrew noun for wickedness uses the feminine gender. To balance the picture, it is women who are often used to represent good and to dispose of wickedness!

To those who first heard this vision, there is no doubt that they would have understood it as a call for holiness and for a commitment to the high standards of morality that God demanded. Failure to respond to God's gracious call would result in further chastening. The challenge remains to this day. We are free to choose whether we allow sin to master us, or by God's grace, we allow him to master sin in us.

On the cross of Calvary the Lord Jesus dealt once and for all with the sin question (compare Psalm 103:12; Isaiah 53:4–6; Hebrews 9:26–28), but we must choose to be done with sin. The apostle Paul put it this way,

In the same way, count yourselves dead to sin, but alive to God in Christ Jesus. Therefore do not let sin reign in your mortal body so that you obey its evil desires. Do not offer the parts of your body to sin, as instruments of wickedness, but rather offer yourselves to God, as those who have been brought from death to life; and offer the parts of your body to him as instruments of righteousness. For sin shall not be your master, because you are not under law, but under grace (Romans 6:11–14).

Zechariah the prophet and Paul the apostle are saying the same thing. When God's people go out into the world, we are confronted with an awesome situation. Both God and sin are looking for weapons to use. God doesn't work without people. If he wants the message made known he gets a person to speak it. If he wants a deed done, he gets a person to do it. It is the same with sin; sin is looking for people who will by their words or example seduce others into wickedness. It is as if prophet and apostle are saying, 'In this world there is an eternal battle between sin and God; choose your side'. We are faced with the tremendous alternative of making ourselves weapons in the hand of God, or weapons in the hand of sin.

Questions

1. What is your reaction to knowing that God's got the measure of our sin?
2. What does the vision of the woman in the basket reveal about the power of wickedness as compared to the power of God? Discuss what you understand by being free to choose sides in the struggle.
3. What evidence can you call to mind that confirms that God disciplines those he loves?

'The country of Babylonia' (5:11)

Wickedness is removed to this place, which can also be translated, 'land of Shinar'. This is the place where the tower of Babel was built and throughout Scripture, from earliest times, it has been understood as referring to those who are against God's way (see Genesis 11:1–9). It is an appropriate home for sin. The prophet sees it as belonging back in Babylon and not in Judah and Jerusalem. The idolatry of Babylon was once and for all to be separated from the worship of the God of Israel. Unlike the fourth vision in which Joshua is relieved of his filthy garments, this vision is concerned with the truth that wickedness, often hidden, is a power which must be reckoned with, never underestimated, but removed by the aid of God's immediate authority. Behind all this remains the eternal truth that the nation or the person whose wickedness is undealt with cannot escape the chastening and the judgment of God.

Zechariah 6:1–8

Chariots of fire

God is on the move and although stormy times are inevitable, he will bring in his kingdom of peace.

Like the first vision of the night, so this last vision features horses of various colours. On this occasion they are seen pulling chariots out from between two mountains of bronze  (6:1–3). The prophet is informed by the interpreting angel that the chariots symbolize the four spirits, or the four winds of God flying towards the north, south, east and west. The result is very satisfying; there is rest for the Spirit of God, a picture of order and peace around the world.

God's sovereign power

This vision helps us to understand something of the sovereignty of God. In Psalm 104: 3–4, we read, 'He makes the clouds his chariot and rides on the wings of the wind. He makes winds his messengers, flames of fire his servants.' The natural elements of cloud, wind and fire are seen as instruments in God's hands. So here in Zechariah's vision, the chariots symbolize God's sovereign control over the whole earth. Not just over nature, but nations as well.

In the first vision the horsemen were seen reconnoitring the whole earth, but in this last vision they are doing even more. Now they are sent out from between these bronze mountains that symbolize the gates of heaven to restore order. Heaven's kingdom is going to be established in the four corners of the earth.

We observe the black horse is going north, the white horse west and the dappled horse south. We are left to assume that the red horse is going east, but we are specifically told that the black horse and chariot travelling north, successfully establishes a time of peace. The point here is plain, if the north can be conquered, so could every other nation of the world. The road north ran first through Syria and then east to Babylon (see map on p. 19). Babylon as we have seen previously, stood for lasting antagonism to God's purposes, but here they are brought into line. God is sovereignly in control. I often say, 'If the Lord can save John James, he can save anyone'. Zechariah was saying, if Babylon could be mastered, then any power can be brought under his authority.

God's kingdom established

Jesus commenced his ministry by preaching, 'Repent, for the kingdom of heaven is near' (Matthew 4:17). Here was a king declaring and inaugurating his kingdom. Throughout the course of his earthly ministry he explained what he meant by his kingdom – the rule of God must be observed if we are to know peace in our lives, homes and between nations (Matthew 5:1–10). Pilate put a label on the cross, acknowledging Jesus to

85

be the King of the Jews (Luke 23:38). At his coronation, John sees him as riding a white horse and 'on his robe and on his thigh he has his name written, 'KING OF KINGS AND LORD OF LORDS' (Revelation 19:16).

All of this is envisaged by Zechariah; see the stallion straining at the leash (6:7) and understand this zeal as the prayer Jesus encourages us to pray, 'Your kingdom come, your will be done on earth as it is in heaven' (Matthew 6:10).

Zechariah foresaw the day that the apostle Paul describes, 'Then the end will come, when he hands over the kingdom to God the Father after he has destroyed all dominion, authority and power. For he must reign until he has put all of his enemies under his feet' (1 Corinthians 15:24–25). After the mighty acts of judgment on the earth, the King of Kings will establish his kingdom and reign as Prince of Peace.

The effect of the four spirits (winds) blowing in all directions is pictured in the Old Testament as the whirlwind. Nahum speaks of the Lord who has his way in the whirlwind and the storm (Nahum 1:3). The winds are God's chariots, seen again in Jeremiah (4:13). God comes with his chariots like a whirlwind (Isaiah 66:15). The wind is the breath of God (Job 37:9, 10). The wind rends the mountains (1 Kings 19:11) and withers the grass (Isaiah 40:7–24) and dries up the stream, the river and the sea (Nahum 1:4; Psalm 18:15).

The whirlwind is often associated with 'The day of the Lord' when all God's enemies would be destroyed (Psalm 83:13; Amos 1:14; Jeremiah 23:19; 30:23; Hosea 13:15; Jeremiah 49:36). In his book *Storm Warning* (Word Publishing, 1993), Billy Graham uses this very imagery to describe what is happening all over the world today. He concludes his book with this explanation, 'The purpose of this storm warning has not been to frighten or alarm people without reason. I have not written these things to cause panic or to create uncertainty, but to offer the bright hope of Jesus Christ as the one who will indeed bring a new and glorious dawn to all mankind.'

We cannot always discern the sovereignty of God in natural

disasters or in international upheaval, but we share the prophets' faith that nothing happens without God's knowledge and consent. All things are moving towards the climax of the ages, God's kingdom coming on earth.

Questions

---

1. What evidence do we have that God deals with us all personally? Each share.
2. From the vision of the four chariots, what is revealed about God's knowledge and control of affairs of all nations?
3. In all of the eight visions angels feature. How do they have influence on human power structures? Why is this good news for those who feel powerless living under evil regimes?

Angels

Angels are referred to throughout the series of eight visions. The term 'angel' means 'messenger'. The word most frequently used throughout Zechariah's prophecy to describe God, is 'The LORD Almighty' which is translated in the Authorized Version as 'The LORD of hosts'. This name of God points to the existence of angelic beings. In Psalm 148:2 in the familiar literary use of parallelism, 'angels' and 'heavenly host' are seen to be one and the same. Similarly, the Old Testament expression, 'Holy ones' may often be read in this way too. Thus angels are understood to be the Lord's army.

Scripture accords to angels a position of authority over the created and historical order, including responsibility for children (Matthew 18:10); protection of God's people (Psalm 34:7); involvement in international affairs (Daniel 10:13; 10:20–11:10); and participation in the judgment of God (Revelation 15–16). Consistent

87

with such authority, a hierarchy of power may be detected among the angels, Michael being described as a prince, an archangel with special authority (Daniel 10:13–21; 12:1; Jude 9; Revelation 12:7).

Angels were created holy (Genesis 1:31; Jude 6). But after a period of probation some fell from their state of innocence (2 Peter 2:4; Jude 6). Scripture is silent regarding the time of their fall, but it is clear that it occurred before the fall of man (for Satan deceived Eve in the garden of Eden) and that it was due to a deliberate, self-determined rebellion against God, as a result of which they lost their original state. They became corrupt and were confirmed in evil. Some were 'Cast down to hell' where they are held in chains until the day of judgment (2 Peter 2:4); while others were left free and they opposed the work of God.

Angels had a significant part to play in the life and ministry of Jesus Christ. They made their appearance in connection with his birth to Mary, to Joseph and to the shepherds. After the wilderness temptation of Christ they ministered to him (Matthew 4:11); an angel strengthened him in the garden (Luke 22:43); an angel rolled away the stone from the tomb (Matthew 28:2–7); and angels were with him at the ascension (Acts 1:10).

As for the fallen angels, it is clear that their principle purpose is to oppose God and to frustrate his purposes. The word 'Satan' which we came across in an earlier vision of Zechariah, shows him to be the adversary of God and the accuser of men and women. Fallen angels oppose good angels in their work (Daniel 10:12, 13). They hinder our temporal and eternal welfare by a limited control over nature (Job 1:12, 13, 19; 2:7); by afflicting disease (Luke 13:11, 16; Acts 10:38; 2 Corinthians 12:7); by tempting us to sin (Matthew 4:3; John 13:27; 1 Peter 5:8); and by spreading false doctrine (1 Kings 22:21–23; 2 Thessalonians 2:2; 1 Timothy 4:1). They cannot, however, exercise over human beings any moral power independent of the human will and whatever power they have is limited by the permissive will of God.

Scripture shows that holy angels will continue in the service of God whilst fallen angels will have their part in the lake of fire (Matthew 25:41).

THE SYMBOLIC
CROWNING OF
JOSHUA

Zechariah 6:9-15

Zechariah 6:9–15

Crown him!

Jesus shall take the highest honour . . .

The writer of the epistle to the Hebrews says, 'In the past God spoke to our forefathers through the prophets at many times and in various ways . . .' (Hebrews 1:1). So far we  have seen the prophet Zechariah speak God's word through preaching and visions. He now employs another way of speaking God's word, by the use of a type or a sign, which many witnessed and understood to be a prediction of the coming Messiah in the dual role of priest and king.

The ceremony (6:9–11)

The prophet had to visit a certain Josiah to meet a group of visitors who were acting as a delegation from the exiles in Babylon. They had brought gifts of silver and gold as a contribution towards the cost of the rebuilding work. From this silver and gold, Zechariah says a crown was to be made that would be placed symbolically on the head of Joshua the high priest, before being placed in the completed temple as a constant reminder of this prophecy (6:11–14).

At this point, the text becomes obscure and commentators

love to speculate; were there one or two crowns? Was Zerubbabel the governor crowned as well as Joshua? Historically you might have expected Zerubbabel to be mentioned here because he was a prince of royal descent, but that is to miss the point of the *symbolic* crowning of Joshua. He who bore the same name as the coming Messiah (as mentioned the Hebrew name Joshua is the name Jesus in the Greek language) prefigures the dual role of the Messiah as priest and king.

There was no way that an actual coronation could have taken place. Jerusalem in Judah was a Persian colony and it would have suffered the wrath or at least the displeasure of the emperor in Babylon and certainly stop the flow of supplies coming through.

Joshua the high priest was chosen in the providence of God as a type of Christ, a king and priest after the order of Melchizedek (the priest-king who appears mysteriously in Genesis 14:18–20. His significance is explained in Hebrews 7:1–17). It was divine wisdom that advised the crowning of Joshua, rather than Zerubbabel.

The significance (6:12–15)

The fact that the coronation was symbolic and typical is clear from the fact that the crown had to be placed in the temple awaiting the true king. It is reminiscent of Excalibur, the legendary sword of King Arthur, which he drew easily from a rock where it was held fast until the moment came for him to claim it.

The significance of the symbolic crowning of Joshua is that it promises that Messiah will come and here we are introduced to his title, task, throne and triumph.

▶ Messiah's title (compare 6:12, 3:8; Jeremiah 23:5, 33:15; Isaiah 4:2)

▶ Messiah's task (compare 6:13; Matthew 16:18; 1 Peter 2:5; Ephesians 2:21)

▶ Messiah's throne (compare 6:13; Hebrews 7:1–22)

▶ Messiah's triumph (compare 6:15; Isaiah 2:2ff; 19:23ff; with 2:11; 8:22; Acts 2:39; 10:35)

Such a revelation calls for a response from God's people.

The challenge

'This will happen if you diligently obey the LORD your God' (6:15). The prophet left his hearers in no doubt that if they wanted to see these prophecies fulfilled, then they needed to live as covenant people. It was a call for diligent obedience as indeed did the ancient law of God (compare Deuteronomy 17:10–11). The New Testament confirms that the most important aspect of the Christian life is obedience. As we obey we move forward. Our progress in the Christian life will always be in proportion to our obedience. You don't have to be famous, clever, or rich to impact the lives of others, you just have to be obedient.

I find it fascinating that in this passage we are introduced to three men who are otherwise anonymous in the annals of human history: Heldai, Dobijah and Jedaiah. They have taken a long journey from their community in Babylon to visit Jerusalem, bringing greetings and gifts. They could hardly have known when they set out the use to which their gifts would be put and the significance of their willingness to make this journey. You may never know the significance of your obedience, or where it will lead to.

It's doubtful if you have ever heard before of Edward Kimball for he was an ordinary man, a Sunday school teacher, who one day was prompted to witness to a shoe salesman in Boston USA. He nervously walked around outside the shoe shop waiting until no-one else was in the store. He went in and on that day in 1858, he led Dwight L. Moody to the Lord. Tens of thousands came to faith through the ministry of Mr Moody, but that's not the end of the story.

Moody came to England and met F. B. Meyer, who was already an effective Bible teacher, but now through this encounter he was stirred to evangelism and led thousands to Christ. F. B. Meyer led one particular student to the Lord, called J. Wilbur Chapman, who also led thousands to Christ. In his evangelistic ministry he employed a base-ball player in the USA called Billy Sunday, who also led many amazing crusades with great effect. One of those crusades was held in North Carolina USA. That mission enthused a group of business men to hold another crusade and invite Mordecai Ham to conduct it. In his meetings a young man received Christ as his Saviour. You might have heard of him – Billy Graham. It all began with Edward Kimball's obedience in obscurity. You may never know the influence that you have. That's God's business, but yours is to obey diligently.

Questions

1. What will happen if we 'diligently' obey the Lord? What may happen if we deliberately disobey him?
2. Look up Ephesians 2:13, 19–22 together with Hebrews 10:12–14 and discuss how Jesus Christ fulfils the predictions of Zechariah in this passage.
3. What do you understand as the missionary task of the church in the phrase, 'Those who are far away will come and help to build the temple of the LORD' (Zechariah 6:15)? What is your local church doing to help bring this to pass?

TWO SERMONS
OF ZECHARIAH

Zechariah 7:1-8:23

Zechariah 7:1–7

Why fast?

It is better not to fast than to do it with wrong motives.

The fifty years commemoration services and events marking the end of World War II seemed to some people to go on and on, especially for those who were too young for it to have personal meaning. In fact there were special fifty years commemorations spread over a five-year period, from the Battle of Britain Events in 1990 through to VE Day and VJ Day in 1995.

It was just before the 'Tribute and Promise Service' to mark the VJ Day in August 1995 that a couple of young people came to see me to ask, 'Should we continue to commemorate these events?'

I have related this story, not to discuss the issue of commemorating various wars long after they have ended, but to illustrate the context of Zechariah chapters 7 and 8. The two chapters should be read together, because they both constitute the Lord's reply through the prophet to the question asked, 'Should I mourn and fast in the fifth month, as I have done for so many years?' (7:3).

Behind the question asked

This day of fasting and mourning commemorated the destruction of the temple in 586 BC, seventy years earlier (see Jeremiah 52:12, 13). It was one of four fast days marking events connected with the fall of the city to Nebuchadnezzar which are described in 2 Kings 25.

- ► The fast in the fourth month marked the breach in the wall of Jerusalem (25:4).

- ► The fast in the fifth month marked the burning of the temple (25:8–9).

- ► The fast in the seventh month marked the murder of Gedaliah (25:25).

- ► The fast in the tenth month marked the beginning of the Babylonian siege of the city (25:1).

Although not in the chapter we are studying now, it should be noted that later in the Lord's reply (8:19) the people were freed from the necessity to fast on those days; instead they were to celebrate, not mourn! The Lord confirmed the presupposition of the question. It is futile commemorating the destruction of the temple, when for two years you have been rebuilding it. That is surely a call for celebration.

The question answered with more questions

The Lord's initial response was to get the prophet to put three questions of his own which reveal the true purpose of fasting.

1. Fasting should involve personal examination

'Was it really for me that you fasted?' (7:5). Check your motives. Why are you mourning and fasting? For the Jew there was only one compulsory fast and that was the Day of Atonement (Leviticus 16:31). The Scribes and Pharisees, however, kept on imposing upon themselves more and more days of fasting. By the time of Jesus, it was two fast days a week, Mondays and Thursdays (Luke 18:12). The Lord Jesus found it necessary to expose them for their play-acting and hypocrisy. How we need to watch such exhibitionism in our hearts and lives. What matters is not what men see, but rather what God sees. We may have to deny ourselves of food, sleep, and recreational times, in order to get alone with God to examine our hearts in the light of his word and in the atmosphere of prayer, but we need to have the right motives for so doing.

2. Fasting should involve personal renunciation

This is seen in the second question posed by the Lord, 'And when you were eating and drinking, were you not just feasting for yourselves?' (7:6). It might seem strange that feasting, not fasting is referred to here. This is to highlight the underlying problem. Eating and drinking satisfies human needs, just as fasting may, but fasting should be directed to the glory of God, not self-gratification. They are challenged about the question of self-denial or personal renunciation.

It is quite clear from the study of the subject of fasting that this has to do with the idea of abstaining from food, but it wasn't essentially limited just to this. The word seems to symbolize all forms of self-denial and therefore has a higher spiritual purpose. It means denying ourselves that which the flesh craves that we may more earnestly live for the Lord. We may need times of fasting and quiet, waiting upon God in order to see ourselves as we really are. If we would really please God, then we must be ready to forgo all manner of self-indulgence – things that in and of themselves are perfectly legitimate – in order that we might give ourselves to walking more closely with God.

3. Fasting should involve personal re-dedication

The third question challenges the citizens of Jerusalem as to how they had used their fast days. My paraphrase of this verse would be, 'Don't you remember what the prophet said at the time?' (7:7). The implication being that the sinful attitudes of their forefathers had led to their failure and the fall of the city. Their fasts were undertaken on account of their sufferings; their sufferings were caused by their sins. So then, their sins were the origin of their fast. Let them remove sin from their midst, then fasting would be unnecessary. One of the reasons why our acts of dedication are not as lasting as they might be, is that we don't take time to get alone with God. This is not to suggest that dedication cannot be real without fasting, but it certainly will not be deep unless there is that disciplined self-denial to spend more time alone with God.

In this respect, fasting means much more than abstinence from food, or anything else. It is to enable us to spend adequate time with God for personal examination, renunciation and re-dedication.

Fasting is still applicable to believers today. There are no specific instructions given as to when Christians are to fast. This is left entirely to the discretion of the individual believer. It is true that this holy exercise has been abused throughout the centuries. The answer to abuse is not non-use but right-use. Christian history has ample evidence of the proper use of fasting, and surely it is time that the Christian church restored this religious exercise to its true biblical setting and purpose (see Matthew 6:16–18; 9:14–17).

Questions

1. What should be our motives for fasting? What experience do you have of fasting personally?
2. When, if ever, do you think the church should fast together locally, nationally, or globally?
3. Do public observances (for instance silence in remembrance of those who have died) achieve anything of value?

Fasting

It is clear from the word of God and from a study of history that fasting has been practised throughout the centuries.

- The patriarchs fasted (Exodus 34:28).

- The prophets fasted (1 Kings 19:8; Ezra 10:6; Daniel 10:3).

- Our Lord Jesus Christ fasted (Matthew 4:2).

- The apostles fasted (Acts 9:9; 2 Corinthians 11:27).

- Leaders in the early church fasted (Acts 13:2; 14:23; 27:33).

- Throughout church history great leaders fasted e.g., Francis of Assisi, Savonarola, Martin Luther, the Reformers John Calvin and John Knox among others, and later John Wesley, Jonathan Edwards and Charles Finney. This subject of fasting is a truth which runs consistently throughout the Bible.

Zechariah 7:8–14

Justice and mercy not fasting

God seeks justice, mercy and compassion more than the observance of religious ritual.

If the people had used fasting for the purpose designed (see last study) they would have remembered the cause and effect of the fall of Jerusalem. It was because their forefathers had refused to hear God's call for justice that disaster had fallen on them. The inference was clear, obedience would have spared them all this trouble. This is a repetition of the teaching in 1:2–6. The lesson to be learned from the exile was a positive one. Every healthy society needs a moral code and the Lord has provided it and it should be observed. In these verses there is a familiar pattern.

The prophets' challenge (7:9–10)

This is the summary teaching of the prophets in the pre-exile period, described in verse 12 as 'The words that the LORD Almighty had sent by his Spirit through the earlier prophets'. The pre-exilic prophets refer to Isaiah, Jeremiah, Hosea, Amos and Micah. They brought a very formidable fourfold challenge (7:9–10):

▶ *Administer true justice.* This would obviously refer to the decisions of the courts. It involves the recovery of equity and peace when there has been injustice and discord, if it is to be 'true justice' (compare Psalm 76:9; Hosea 2:19). However, administering true justice extends beyond the court-house, for too often God's people individually and corporately judge others harshly, which they would rightly condemn in others (see Matthew 7:1–2).

▶ *Show mercy and compassion to one another.* Micah put it like this, 'What does the LORD require of you? To act justly and to love mercy and to walk humbly with your God' (Micah 6:8). 'To love mercy' is a divine requirement. The Hebrew word for 'mercy' implies the ability to get right inside the other person's skin, until we can see things with his eyes, think things with his mind, and feel things with his feelings. This is just what God did in order to show us mercy, he became flesh and dwelt among us: seeing with our eyes, thinking with our minds and feeling with our hearts (see John 1:14). How challenging this is! How remote and aloof we often are in the work of God. We know little or nothing of involvement, identification and tenderness. God have mercy on us!

▶ *Do not oppress the widow, or the fatherless, the alien or the poor.* The list here includes those who have no-one to stand by them, or to speak up for them, and therefore are all too open to exploitation. The very use of the words, 'Do not' implies that this is the very thing that usually happens. The people of God certainly must not.

▶ *In your hearts do not think evil of each other.* Sin is not only what we do, it's what's in the heart, the unseen and the unspoken plans made in the secret places.

What a concise and comprehensive range of ethical teachings we have here. Without attention to these imperatives any fasting would be a mere ritual, which as the history of Judah had shown, would only lead to moral and spiritual disaster. Why remember to observe a fast if you forget the reasons that precipitated it.

The people's contempt (7:11–12)

Use your imagination as you read these verses. What picture of these people do you see from what they did with their backs, ears and hearts? What is suggested to you as you read of a heart that's as hard as flint (7:12)?

Turning their backs or literally, 'a stubborn shoulder', is more than giving the Lord the cold shoulder. It speaks of wilful disobedience and resistance. The phrase 'turned their backs' would be used to describe an ox that refused to receive the yoke.

'They stopped their ears', means to deliberately refuse to listen to the word of God.

'They made their hearts as hard as flint' (7:12). They stifled their emotions, making their hearts as hard as a flint. They were adamant, stubborn and unyielding. They would not under any circumstance allow the word of God to penetrate their consciences.

The Lord's chastening (7:13–14)

'So the LORD Almighty was very angry ... "I scattered them with a whirlwind among all the nations, where they were strangers. The land was left so desolate behind them that no-one could come or go. This is how they made the pleasant land desolate."' We need to keep reminding ourselves of the context of this teaching which was as a result of the question asked about fasting (7:3). The prophet is speaking now to the descendants of those rebellious people. He was trying to help them recognize the real issue in the question about continuing to fast for past tragedies. God called to his people and found no response. In their distress they cried to him and were given no answer, except the events which followed, eloquently testifying to God's displeasure as they were blown away like chaff in a whirlwind. Zechariah may not have answered the original question directly, but he had taken up the very essence of ritual in the heart of the worshipper, which was that outward form of religious activity was useless and lifeless without an accompanying spirit of obedience, confession and repentance.

Questions

1. Spend time visualizing the picture of a people whose backs, ears and hearts are described in 7:11. Discuss the challenge it presents to us.
2. Why should we 'administer true justice, show mercy and compassion to one another'?
3. Who are the oppressed, the widows, the fatherless, the aliens and the poor in our society? How can we help them?

Inspiration of the Scripture

'The words that the LORD Almighty had sent by his Spirit through the earlier prophets.' (7:12). Perhaps nowhere else is the idea of inspiration so clearly stated as here. This reference to the Spirit as the unifying influence behind the prophets' preaching is almost unique in the Old Testament literature. We do see it again in Nehemiah 9:30, 'By your Spirit you admonished them through your prophets.' It is a timely reminder. As Peter put it, 'above all; you must understand that no prophecy of Scripture came about by the prophets' own interpretation. For prophecy never had its origin in the will of man, but men spoke from God as they were carried along by the Holy Spirit.' (2 Peter 1:20–21) It is a fact that the Bible was written by people. God chose about forty human writers and he used them to write the sixty-six books of the Bible, but it is important to notice that their writing didn't originate 'in the will of man'. What they wrote was not a concoction of their own ideas, and it was not the result of human imagination, insight or speculation. The Bible was, and is inspired by the Holy Spirit. This is clearly brought out, 'men spoke from God as they were carried along by the Holy Spirit.' The Holy Spirit is the divine author and he inspired the writers as they wrote. The Bible is fully and completely inspired by God, and is therefore wholly reliable.

Zechariah 8:1–23

Fasts into festivals

The manifest presence of God calls for celebration and a change of life.

The context of this second of two sermons is in response to the question 'Should I mourn and fast?' (7:3). The reply is given ultimately, 'The fasts of the fourth, fifth, seventh and tenth months will become joyful and glad occasions and happy festivals for Judah. Therefore love truth and peace' (8:19). The Lord said that for them at that time it was an occasion of feasting, not fasting (compare Mark 2:18–20).

The prophet has come to the point in his revelation where he saw beyond the desolation to restoration; beyond the chastening of God to the return of all the people to the land and the establishing of God's kingdom where citizens love truth and peace (8:19).

The Hebrew prophets had always caught glimpses of the coming glory, the fullness of which is seen in the reign of Jesus as King (John 1:14). These men of God saw the city of God in the distance. They saw the walls of that city. They saw the way of life when the city was built and the Kingdom of God established there. Among all such visions there is none, in my opinion, more graphic or full of suggestion than that which is in the passage before us. Zechariah saw a city where the kingdom of heaven had come on earth. Moreover, he was absolutely certain it would come to pass because of the zeal of Jehovah (8:2). God's jealousy or zeal is to be understood in relation to the covenant. This verse suggests a surge of feeling such as would be seen in the face of a person red with emotion. It is as though God can restrain himself no longer despite the obstinacy and the sin of his people. So great is God's love for Zion that he announces his intention to return and dwell in Jerusalem, whose sad fortunes will be reversed (8:3).

An idyllic picture is painted of a restored Jerusalem.

The name of the city (8:3)

- *The city of truth* i.e., the place where belief and behaviour, creed and conduct go hand in hand (compare Isaiah 2:16; Jeremiah 3:17).

- *The Holy Mountain* i.e., a city set apart and distinct from all other places.

The nature of life in the city (8:4ff)

- 'Once again men and women of ripe old age will sit in the streets of Jerusalem, each with a cane in hand because of his age' (8:4).

- 'The city street will be filled with boys and girls playing there' (8:5).

The prophet recognized that this was an incredible vision. The Lord says that what might surprise us doesn't surprise him. Old men and women should be able to feel safe on the streets. Boys and girls should be able to play together in the parks. A community is no community unless both old and young can live together harmoniously and at peace. A community without older people or children is an incomplete and an impoverished society. However, a community that has old and young, but cannot live together in peace, falls short of God's ideal.

The tragedy of our day is that there are few places in the world that are safe for children or old people. The vulnerable are often exploited and abused which serves to demonstrate how far short we fall of kingdom standards.

Beyond the joy of the elderly and the young being present together, Zechariah sees the restoration of the entire community. At the moment the comparatively empty city lying in ruins (see Nehemiah 11:1) was an unlikely place for such a happy scene. But those still in exile would return, the population would grow and God's covenant with his people would be renewed. The Lord could see their potential even if they couldn't. 'I will bring them back to live in Jerusalem; they will be my people, and I will be faithful and righteous to them as their God' (8:8).

Incentives to be strong (8:9ff)

Twice in these verses we read 'Let your hands be strong' (8:9, 13). This is a repetition of Haggai's earlier message with the same emphasis providing incentives to be strong:

- The satisfaction of a job well done i.e., the completion of the temple (8:9)

- The security that comes with peace with your neighbours (8:10)

- The successful harvests that are assured (8:12)

- The source of blessing to other nations (8:13).

The message is plain – the kingdom where God is seen to be present is worth working for, so – go for it!

There follows a repetition of the earlier message, the moral and ethical standards of God's people (compare 8:16–17 and 7:8–9). Then we have the explicit answer to the question of fasting (8:18–19) which we have studied already (see *Fasting* p. 100). Sufficient to say that celebration is the order of the day, but it needed to be a worship that was lived out in their daily lives, concluding with the phrase, 'Love truth and peace' (8:19).

Truth and peace were to be the hallmarks of the redeemed community. They still are. The truth of God must rule our heads (Ephesians 4:23–25) and the peace of God must rule our hearts and our heads (Philippians 4:7). Honesty and harmony are goals that we must never forget.

The final incentive provided to the citizens of Jerusalem is a fitting climax to the final part of this book of Zechariah. It is a development of verse 13 which said that the people of God will be a blessing to the Gentile nations. There will be such a magnet-like attraction among the people of God, that many will want to come and join the worship.

Contrast the promise, 'I will return to Zion and dwell in Jerusalem' (8:3) with the prediction that the Gentiles will say to the Jews, 'Let us go with you, because we have heard that God is with you' (8:23). The manifest presence of God will always have this effect. The community at Corinth may have had its problems, but the Apostle Paul said that when the unbeliever comes into their worship, they 'will fall down and worship God exclaiming God is really among you' (1 Corinthians 14:25).

It's good to be part of a community of faith that is being renewed and biblical standards are being restored, but that will never be enough. What we need here is a heaven-sent Holy Spirit revival. Maybe we do need to fast and pray, that we might know again the manifest presence of God.

Questions

1. Discuss the difference between the omnipresence of God and his manifest presence.
2. Observing your local church, would you say it was time for fasting or celebrating? Why?
3. The picture of senior citizens at rest and children at play in the streets (8:4–5) is difficult to imagine in many of our cities and towns today. What's gone wrong with the world? What is the answer to the fear in the community?

The remnant (8:6)

The remnant are those people who remain faithful to God and his covenant despite the surrounding pressures and problems of life. At first, the word as used in the Scriptures denoted a part of a family or clan left from slaughter, but later came to be applied to the spiritual kernel of the nation who would survive God's judgment and become the germ of the new people of God. Thus Micah saw the returning glory of God (2:12; 5:7). Zephaniah saw the triumph of this remnant (2:4–7) as did Zechariah here. Isaiah named a son Shear Jashub which means 'A remnant returns' (7:3).

In the New Testament, the Greek words used in Romans (9:27; 11:5) have the same underlying meaning. The promise of God that there will always be a remnant, who remain in any given situation, has the implication of judgment and hope: God will preserve. It is by the grace of God that we are saved and kept (compare Jude 1 and 24).

'I will save my people' (8:7). To 'save' in Hebrew usually means deliverance from captivity or bondage. Probably two ideas are brought together here. Certainly the remnant represented God's saving mercy. Yet in delivering a remnant, God was in fact saving his people from the possibility of extinction by bringing them home from the far flung corners of the earth, to receive the renewed covenant promise.

Judah and Israel (8:13)

Judah was the southern half of the land of Israel which split from the north after the death of King Solomon (1 Kings 12:20) and it included the city of Jerusalem. The tribes occupying this area of Israel were Judah, part of Benjamin which was incorporated into Judah (the other part joining the northern kingdom) and Simeon. It was viewed by biblical writers as the more Godly of the two kingdoms because it remained loyal to the house of David, God's chosen king. As the majority of those who returned from Babylon came from Judah, the word 'Jew' came into common use to describe those who came from any part of Israel.

The significance of Jewish clothes

'In those days ten men from all languages and nations will take firm hold of one Jew by the hem of his robe and say . . .' (8:23). 'Ten men' is a figure indicating completeness (compare Leviticus 26:26; 1 Samuel 1:8). 'From all languages and nations': the word used here was and often still is, a term used by the Jew as a contemptuous reference to the non-Jew. 'Will take firm hold of one Jew by the hem of his robe': the verb 'hold' indicates an impulsive, but deeply sincere action. For a possible illustration, we remember the woman who reached out to touch the hem of the garment of Jesus (see Matthew 9:21). On the outer garment worn by Jews there were four tassels as instructed in the law (see Numbers 15:37–41). They consisted of four threads, passing through the four corners of the garment and meeting in eight. One of the threads was longer than the others. It was twisted seven times around the others and a double knot formed; and eight times and then eleven times, then thirteen times. The thread and the knots stood for the five books of the law. The idea of the fringe was twofold. It was meant to identify a Jew as a Jew, and as a member of the chosen people, no matter where he was; and it was meant to remind a Jew every time he put on and took off his clothes that he belonged to God. It was the tassel on the robe of Jesus that was touched by the woman with the issue of blood. It was this same tassel that is referred to in Zechariah's prophecy.

THE FUTURE OF
THE KINGDOM

Zechariah 9 – 11

Zechariah 9:1–17

Rejoicing in Jerusalem

**God's covenant people have
a great deal to rejoice about.**

From this point in Zechariah's prophecy there
is a change in style and substance; there are
no explicit references to the prophet himself
and all the messages are now undated.
Nevertheless, the two sections of Zechariah's book certainly
belong together. This second part develops a number of the key
issues touched on previously. Chapters 9 – 11 refer to the future
of the Messianic kingdom and chapters 12 – 14 refer to the future
of the Messiah himself. The first eight chapters related particularly to the scene of the rebuilding of the temple, whilst in the
second section there is a more pronounced apocalyptic feel and a
stronger Messianic flavour. Both parts, however, have in common the attention paid to the Lord's plan of deliverance.

This second section can be divided, as we have said, into
another two parts, each of which is introduced by the words 'An
Oracle' (9:1 and 12:1). This word can equally be translated
'burden'. The term usually appears in connection with a
prophet's declaration of the word of God. It describes a burden
placed upon a prophet's shoulders, a message that although not
easy, he was constrained nevertheless to deliver.

Chapter 9 can be divided into three sections (1–8; 9–10; 11–17).

Invasion (9:1–8)

For God's kingdom to be established, rival kingdoms have to be dislodged. The prophet foretold the preservation of the city of Jerusalem (9:8) in the very days when Syria to the north, Phoenicia to the west and Philistia to the south-west would be overcome by the enemy. All this would be the Lord's doing. This prophecy was to a large extent fulfilled by the coming of Alexander the Great. In 333 BC he captured Damascus and Sidon and after a siege of seven months Tyre itself. He then marched against Gaza and razed it to the ground. In the course of this campaign he passed Jerusalem more than once but never attacked it. Thus according to the prophecy of Zechariah the city was preserved for the coming of the true king.

Inauguration (9:9–10)

God's invasion of the neighbouring nations would set the stage for the restoration of Zion's king (9:9–10). These two verses are well known from the New Testament (compare Matthew 21:4f; John 12:14f). The gospel writers had no hesitation in saying that this prophecy was fulfilled in the triumphal entry of Jesus into Jerusalem. It speaks of the Lord's sovereign rule.

1. The majesty of the king

► *The majesty of his righteousness* (9:9). Repressive governments and heads of state today are rightly being challenged concerning their record of human rights. We long for a righteousness and justice which will be enacted or enforced only when Jesus Christ reigns on the throne of the universe (Isaiah 9:6–7).

► *The majesty of his gentleness* (9:9). The word speaks of his meekness and humility. The greatest moment in history, so far as humility is concerned, was when God contracted to

115

the measure of a woman's womb; when the eternal God was born in time (compare Philippians 2:5–11).

The Lord offers to our imagination a picture of his kingship and style of government, a king who comes amongst us as one who serves.

2. The mastery of the king

A king riding on a donkey was a symbol of gentleness and humility, but it was also a symbol of peace. From Matthew's account of Palm Sunday we learn something of the control that the king exercised. He was the master of the universe; you just sense that mastery as Matthew relates the story of how he commandeered the colt (Matthew 21:2–3) and how he controlled the colt (Matthew 21:6–9). Apparently it takes at least eight weeks to break in a colt and possibly another eight weeks or longer to train the young animal to behave in a crowd. With great rejoicing, singing and shouting, King Jesus rode that colt into the city. What a picture of the control that the Lord wants to exercise over the lives of his kingdom people.

3. The ministry of the king

'See your king comes to you . . . having salvation . . .' (9:9). The purpose for which the Lord Jesus Christ came into the world was to bring salvation to men and women (compare Titus 2:11; Matthew 1:21; Acts 2:21). This world of ours, with all of its tumult, division and injustice, needs not more education, reformation or litigation, but God's salvation.

Intervention (9:11–17)

God is a covenant-keeping God and on the basis of that covenant he will intervene on behalf of his people. The prophet foretold Zion's coming triumph against Greece. The Lord is seen as the warrior and the nation is seen as a weapon in his hand. It is thought that this prophecy was fulfilled in the victory of Judas Maccabaeus over Antiochus Epiphanes in 165 BC (9:13).

All of this is to serve as further encouragement for the people still in exile to return home (9:11–12).

The Lord is also seen as a shepherd (9:16), imagery that becomes very familiar in this second part of Zechariah's prophecy. In feel this passage echoes the pastoral concern of the first eight chapters. The Lord empathizes with his people's suffering and promises strength in areas where there was weakness. It shows the Lord as soldier and shepherd, able to protect and to provide for his people. It reveals God's continuing care for all his people.

Questions

1. The coming of the Messiah was to bring salvation. What does God save us from?
2. What promises are made concerning God's covenant people (verses 11–17)? What do they mean to you?
3. War and peace are themes that run through this chapter. What do you think the Christian view of war and peace is?

Geography

The Land of Hadrach (9:1). Hadrach was the name of a town or district in the neighbourhood of Damascus and Hamath. It is not mentioned anywhere else in the Old Testament.

Damascus (9:1), *Hamath, Tyre and Sidon* (9:2), *Ashkelon, Gaza, Ekron* (9:5). You can locate all these places in Syria, Phoenicia and Philistia mentioned in this passage on the map provided. 'Ekron shall be like the Jebusites' (9:7): Ekron, one of the five principal Philistine townships is promised a peaceful future of co-existence such as afforded the Jebusites, the ancient Canaanite residents of the suburbs of Jerusalem after David had captured that city.

117

Ephraim (9:10). Ephraim here is synonymous with Israel. Ephraim became such a leader in the northern Hebrew kingdom that, in addition to its more common name Israel, the kingdom is also called Ephraim. Ephraim is also the name of a city north of Jerusalem, but here it represents all Israel.

Biblical terms

Daughter of Zion (9:9). 'daughter' is a term which often speaks of severed relationships in the Old Testament (e.g. Isaiah 1:8; Jeremiah 4:31; Lamentations 2:1). However this passage is an exception. By contrast Jerusalem is given the news that the time of waiting is over. The arrival of a king is imminent.

The blood of my covenant (9:11). The actual words 'blood of the covenant' occur only here, in Exodus 24:8 and Mark 14:24. It speaks of the original basis of God's special dealings with his own people. It is not until we enter the New Testament, however, that they assume their total significance.

Waterless pit (9:11). This speaks of Babylon. The prophet is speaking of a dramatic change in the fortunes of the people of God and uses highly colourful language to describe the contrast of freedom from captivity.

How many donkeys?

Riding on a donkey, on a colt, the foal of a donkey (9:9b). Some people ask how many donkeys did the Lord Jesus ride into Jerusalem on, one or two? The presence of two donkeys is the product of Hebrew parallelism, but only a single donkey was used. The Gospel writers, Mark, Luke and John refer to our Lord riding on a colt or a young donkey. It is Matthew's account that refers to a donkey and its colt, but only the colt was ridden. We must be impressed with the Gospel writers' attempt to look for literal interpretation of the text whenever possible.

Zechariah 10:1–12

Restoration of Jerusalem

God's compassion and care for us has its own claim on our lives.

The amazing promises of the last chapter are added to now, but not before a particular responsibility is spelled out, the necessity of praying for God's blessings to come.

The people may feel like 'prisoners from the waterless pit' (9:11) so he now says, 'Ask the LORD for rain' (10:1). It is the Lord alone who can meet our needs at the appropriate time.

The Lord as the good shepherd is the dominant theme running through the next two chapters. The failure of national leaders is contrasted to the care that the Lord promises (10:2–3).

The problems are enumerated

God's people had been like sheep without a shepherd and therefore vulnerable to those who were skilled at manipulating the situation for their own good. The people had been led up a blind alley by:

▶ *Idols [that] speak deceit* (10:2). These were household idols used for divination. You will find a reference to them in

119

Judges 17:5. They are also mentioned by Amos before Israel fell to Assyria.

▶ *Visions that lie* (10:2). These visions by diviners were forbidden in Israel, but they interpreted omens as a way of foretelling the future.

▶ *Dreams that give false comfort* (10:2). Dreamers were false prophets who claimed authoritative dreams.

For such leadership the so-called shepherds were under the judgment of God (10:3). The truth is that we all need to be led but too often we follow the wrong leaders, who are as lost as we are. Lost sheep do not make for good shepherds, but those who are shepherds face a greater judgment than those that they lead.

The promise is emphasized

The good shepherd will come for his flock and restore them to a place of security and significance (10:3). There are two main promises of restoration.

1. The promise of the restoration of good leadership (10:4–5)

The flock of sheep become a mighty army under the leadership of one who will be as secure as a 'cornerstone' or a 'tent peg'; and as strong as a 'battle-bow' or 'great ruler'. This leadership was ultimately to come from the Messiah who is often referred to as the 'cornerstone' (compare Isaiah 28:16; Matthew 21:42; Ephesians 2:20; 1 Peter 2:6). The Lord Jesus is also identified in the New Testament as the good shepherd (John 10).

2. The promise of the restoration of genuine liberation (10:6–12)

The promised victory is emphasized by Jehovah's own promises. Notice: 'I will', and 'they shall' repeated over and over again.

The restoration and redemption promised here is not just to what things were like before they went into Babylon, but it would be even greater than the Exodus from Egypt.

▶ It would involve all Israel of the north and the south (10:6–8).

▶ Things will be better than they had ever been (10:6).

▶ It would be marked by great joy (10:7).

▶ There would be numerical growth (10:8 and 10b).

▶ People will be drawn from all directions (10:9–10).

▶ Their enemies would be overthrown (10:11).

▶ They will be strengthened and in his name make progress (10:12).

Zechariah is looking beyond the restoration of the redeemed community to the new covenant. The redemption (10:8) referred to is more literally translated 'ransom' and it looked forward to the coming of the good shepherd who would lay down his life for his sheep (John 10:11). The good shepherd cares for his sheep and waits for them to call on him to rescue them. His love for us puts a claim on us to reach out to him in prayer.

The chapter begins with an encouragement to pray. 'Ask the LORD for rain in the springtime; it is the LORD who makes the storm clouds. He gives showers of rain to men . . .' (10:1). In the light of God's many mercies, may we make this appropriate response.

> Let it come Oh Lord we pray Thee
> Let the showers of blessing fall
> We are waiting and expecting
> Oh revive the hearts of all.

Questions

1. What idols, diviners and dreamers do people follow today in their desire for help and direction in life?
2. The gospel of Jesus Christ is the good news of freedom to those in bondage. How is your church demonstrating this truth in the community?
3. Why should we pray for the whole world, and in what ways do you think you could become a more effective praying church?

Egypt and Assyria (verses 10–11)

Egypt and Assyria are often mentioned together in Scripture. They were both places where God's covenant people had been taken into slavery and exile. In this passage they are twin symbols of slavery. The returning exiles, however, will overrun the northern and eastern frontiers of the homeland. Nevertheless, both Egypt and Assyria are promised a bright future in partnership with Israel.

In that day there will be a highway from Egypt to Assyria. The Assyrians will go to Egypt and the Egyptians to Assyria. The Egyptians and Assyrians will worship together. In that day Israel will be the third, along with Egypt and Assyria, a blessing on the earth. The LORD Almighty will bless them, saying, 'Blessed be Egypt my people, Assyria my handiwork, and Israel my inheritance.' (Isaiah 19:23–25)

Zechariah 11:1–17

Revelation to Jerusalem

God's grace is always towards his people but he won't allow us to get away with murder.

Verses 1–3 are a poem lamenting the devastation of the historic enemies of Israel and Judah. Some commentators believe that Lebanon and Bashan are mentioned not to identify the nations to be judged, but rather to draw attention to the fact that the famous trees from these regions can be destroyed, and if they can be cut down to size everyone needs to watch out! In verse 6 the people of Palestine are clearly identified as ripe for judgment and the opening verses set the scene for the revelation of God's wrath. In verses 4–17 there are a few clear facts.

- Israel is a picture of a flock of sheep.
- Their leaders are bad shepherds (11:4–6).
- The prophet engages in role play as the Lord's own good shepherd, who is rejected.

The passage is principally an allegory (a symbolic story). It would have a direct application to a historical setting, but no-one is sure what it was. It clearly looked forward to the coming of the good shepherd, the Lord Jesus Christ and his rejection, but it also has an application even beyond that. It speaks to all who exercise pastoral leadership amongst God's people. There are bad and good shepherds and we are all accountable to that chief shepherd of the sheep.

The historic setting

The local leaders had been more like butchers than shepherds (verse 5); they should have protected the sheep, but instead were concerned only with their profitability.

The prophet acting as the shepherd chosen by the Lord (verse 7) has two staffs called 'Favour' and 'Union', and in one month he got rid of three bad shepherds (verse 8). The staffs represent the gracious purposes of God towards all his people. The Lord wants to bless them and desires their unity. Historically he desired the unity of Israel and Judah. The identity of the three shepherds who are disposed of are a mystery, despite attempts to identify them with three historical leaders who were got rid of in the space of a month.

The flock, however, are not impressed with and reject the good shepherd, and the rule of God that he represents (verse 8b). As a revelation of God's wrath, his people are abandoned to the consequences of their rejection of him (compare Romans 1:24, 26, 28). The good shepherd broke the staff called 'Favour', annulling the covenant he had with the flock (verses 10–11). The leaders show their contempt for the prophet (verse 12) and so the Lord instructed him to break the second staff 'union', indicating that there would be no unity between Israel and Judah (verse 14). Even worse was to come in the person of a leader who would exploit the people, but then he himself would suffer the wrath of God (verses 15–17). Again we cannot identify the person historically, but prophetically it may be possible to do so.

The prophetic symbolism

In the light of the New Testament application of this passage we see how it describes the rejection of the Lord Jesus as king. One opinion is that the forest fires (verses 1–3) are a picture of the destruction of Jerusalem by the Romans, following the rejection of Jesus as the anointed king of Israel.

The Lord Jesus possessed the staffs of Favour and Union. He brings to us the grace of God and in him all things will be brought together. He came to his own people but they rejected him (John 1:11). Judas betrayed him for thirty pieces of silver (Matthew 26:15) and then threw the money into the treasury. The chief priests used the money to buy the potter's field (Matthew 27:3–10). The gospel writers clearly applied Zechariah's prophecy to what Judas had done.

In this light verses 15–17 stand as a judgment of the Jewish leaders who conspired against the Lord Jesus. The prophet foresaw the Roman destruction of Jerusalem following the rejection of their true king.

The abiding relevance

The Lord desires to bless his people and is always acting on our behalf. The New Testament application of this passage demonstrates the overruling providence of God. The Jewish leaders and our Lord's own disciples failed him, but God, nevertheless, was fulfilling his purposes supernaturally. 'Hallelujah! For our Lord God Almighty reigns' (Revelation 19:6).

In the light of this truth, how foolish we are to resist the purposes of God. Pastoral leaders particularly should be warned that to whom much is given, much is required.

Be shepherds of God's flock that is under your care, serving as overseers – not because you must, but because you are willing, as God wants you to be; not greedy for money, but eager to serve; not lording it over those entrusted to you, but being examples to the flock. And when the Chief Shepherd appears, you will receive the crown of glory that will never fade away. (1 Peter 5:2–4)

Questions

1. What comparisons can be made with the shepherds of this chapter and the Lord Jesus Christ, the good shepherd, in John 10:10–16?
2. How effective is the pastoral care in your fellowship and how can it be improved?
3. God is at work in all the world. Where can we see his hand in the national and international events around us?

THE FUTURE OF
THE KING

Zechariah 12 - 14

Zechariah 12:1–14

Punishment by Jerusalem

Jesus Christ will be acknowledged as the Messiah and the enemies of God will be destroyed.

The events in this chapter have never known fulfilment; neither at the fall of Jerusalem under Nebuchadnezzar, or Titus; nor at the Maccabean uprising of 165 BC when they  drove the Syrians out of the city. This chapter takes us into the final major section of Zechariah's prophecy. The king spoken of in the previous message, whose rejection was foretold, is now seen coming into his kingdom.

In these final three chapters the phrase 'On that day' is repeated sixteen times with another reference to 'The day of the LORD' (see p. 46). This is apocalyptic writing and Zechariah points to the day to which all human history is moving, a climax of the ages that Christians call the second coming of Jesus Christ.

The destruction of Jerusalem's enemies (12:1–9)

Verses 1–9 picture all the nations of the earth gathering against Jerusalem (verse 3), but against expectations the angel of the Lord leads his people in the great victory (verse 9).

The Lord is described (verse 1)

He is the creator God. He who brought order out of chaos at the beginning will on 'his day' re-establish Paradise lost. Belief in God the creator will always inspire hope in his people, no matter how desperate the situation may appear.

The invasion is described (verses 2–4)

A global conspiracy against the people of God is envisaged, but God is on the side of his people and he makes them:

▶ A cup that sends everyone 'reeling' (verse 2) – the enemies of God will be as incapable as a drunk.

▶ An immovable rock (verse 3) – on which the enemy disables itself.

As a consequence of the people becoming drunk and disabled they panic and act insanely (verse 4) and are doomed to failure.

Judah is described (verses 5–7)

The implication of this chapter is that at first the troops of Judah are against Jerusalem as part of this global conspiracy, but seeing the outcome allies itself to the holy city and becomes a powerful instrument to save the inhabitants of Jerusalem.

The citizens of Jerusalem are described (verses 8–9)

Protected by the Lord himself, even the weakest of God's people are made more than conquerors and an overwhelming victory is experienced.

Christian opinion is divided over whether this passage should be understood literally. Certainly for those who see modern-day Israel as centre-stage in world history and at the same time observe the nations of the world acting together globally, it seems as though the scene is set for such a climax of the ages and the return of our Lord Jesus Christ.

However, the Christian who is not convinced that you need to understand this passage literally, nevertheless sees here a message of encouragement to God's people in every age. The enemies of God, no matter how powerful, or from wherever they emerge, will be overcome and God's kingdom will be established and his anointed king will reign.

Mourning for the one they pierced

Verses 10–14 view the same events, but the great victory described is followed not by rejoicing, but repentance and sorrow. The inhabitants of Jerusalem have killed someone and in due course see that they were responsible.

The writer of the gospel of John had no hesitation in quoting verse 10 as part of his witness to the crucifixion of our Lord Jesus. 'They will look on the one they have pierced.' He said that part of the prophecy was fulfilled (John 19:34–37). As to the effect of what they see, however, that is still to be fulfilled. John wrote, 'Look he is coming with the clouds, and every eye will see him, even those who pierced him, and all the peoples of the earth will mourn because of him. So shall it be!' (Revelation 1:7).

The prophets saw God's anointed King coming in both suffering and in glory. They foresaw Mount Calvary and Mount Zion as two peaks, but only in the light of the New Testament can we see the long valley running between the first and the second comings of Christ. The crucifying and the crowning of the king are seen here in Zechariah's prophecy.

The great sorrow to be expressed is as a result of God's spirit of 'grace and supplication' being poured out on God's people (verse 10). Like all that God accomplishes in his people it is undeserved, so that all the glory goes to him. The whole community share this sense of guilt and grief. It is clearly personal yet corporate repentance, with everyone crying out to God for mercy. This is always the case when God gives grace to his people; they call on his name in prayer.

Whilst this passage speaks principally to the Jews, it is nevertheless true of all sinners. Where there is true repentance for sin, it is because we recognize Christ died for us and because of us.

Questions

1. Why and how does belief in God the creator always inspire hope in his people?
2. What, if anything, is your church doing to prepare for the second coming of Christ?
3. What should the Christian attitude be to the nation of Israel and to the United Nations?

Hadad Rimmon

'The weeping of Hadad Rimmon in the plain of Megiddo' (12:11). Hadad Rimmon is a place in the valley of Megiddo, named after two Syrian gods. It was the place where Josiah king of Judah was wounded and killed (2 Kings 23:29–30) and became a place of mourning. It is also thought, however, that Hadad Rimmon is the name of a fertility god (see 2 Kings 5:18) whose death was mourned annually in the dry season. The scholar F. F. Bruce has also suggested that this ritual may have become linked with the annual memorial for Josiah (see 2 Chronicles 35:25).

Zechariah 13:1–9

Purification of Jerusalem

The coming of the Messiah brings the hope of cleansing from sin and the making of the people of God.

The imagery of this chapter is clear. Zechariah uses the vehicles of prose (verses 1–6), and poetry (verses 7–9) to convey two graphic pictures.

Redeeming the repentant (13:1–6)

In the last chapter, God's people in Jerusalem and Judah displayed evidence of repentance (12:10). Now the Lord provides cleansing from their sin (error) and impurity (ritual impurity). The 'fountain' is identified as the Messiah himself (compare Jeremiah 2:13; Ezekiel 36:25 and John 4:14). William Cowper's hymn, 'There is a fountain filled with blood', expresses the truth well. We all need to come to that fountain for cleansing.

Two specific sins are highlighted that need to be confessed: idolatry (13:2) and hypocrisy (13:3–6).

▶ Idolatry, the worship of a man-made image as if it were a god, had been a persistent corruption of the faith, and still is!

▶ Hypocrisy, pretending to be better than one is, is seen in the false prophets. A distinction is made between the true and false prophets, by linking these false prophets with the phrase, 'spirit of impurity' (13:2). Genuine prophecy is an authentic ministry of the new covenant, but it is always to be linked with holiness. It is inspired by the Holy Spirit (1 Corinthians 2:13ff and 1 John 4:1–6). We must always be on our guard against the corruption of everything that is good and holy.

The shame as well as guilt is shared by parents of the so-called prophet as well as the person himself (13:3–6). The message is one of hope, however, the coming Kingdom will be known by its absolute integrity.

Refining the remnant

In this, Zechariah's last poem, he returns to the theme of the good shepherd. The Lord Jesus leaves us in no doubt about the interpretation and application that we are to make of the passage (Mark 14:27).

▶ The Lord Jesus was the shepherd struck (13:7). This verse is Father God's permission for his son to be struck. 'The man who is close to me' is the king who stands next to God as the one with delegated authority to rule. The idea of the Messiah being struck is seen throughout the prophets (see Micah 5:1; Isaiah 50:6; 53:4, 10).

▶ The disciples of Jesus were the sheep scattered (compare 13:7; Matthew 26:31 and John 16:32). The consequences of the shepherd being struck, however, were to be felt beyond the followers of Jesus to 'the whole land'.

▶ The Jewish nation was struck down and a period of refining began (13:8–9). Within a generation of the crucifixion of Christ, in AD 70, one million Jews died in the battle of

Masada and in Jerusalem. A further half a million died under the Bar Kokhba rebellion of AD 130. From then to the present, the history of the Jewish people has been full of tragedy. With God, however, there is always that doctrine of the remnant and it is seen here in these verses.

The Lord has not left himself without a witness. Disciples of all nations (Jews and Gentiles) are testimony to the fact that through many tribulations God's Kingdom is established. As gold is purified by fire, so too God's people are strengthened by times of trial (verse 9). Moreover, beyond these trials the prophet sees the day when God and his people are reconciled and own each other gladly.

Questions

1. What is the difference between guilt and shame? How does the death of Jesus Christ help us deal with these two emotions?
2. How do idolatry and hypocrisy still threaten the church of Jesus Christ? What safeguards do we have against them?
3. Suffering is compared to the refining of gold by fire. What possible good can come out of such painful experiences? Is the world's suffering (through war, natural disasters, famine and disease) all useless? Does it have any meaning?

Zechariah 14:1–21

Peace for Jerusalem but the plague for its enemies

When the Lord is king over all the earth, everyone will worship him as God and know him by the same name.

 Zechariah is attempting to describe the indescribable as he comes to the ultimate victory of the king, the great day of the Lord, which will be ushered in by Jehovah coming to the Mount of Olives in the person of the king. He conveys the truth that beyond the coming chaos he sees a new world arising from the rubbish of the old.

Chapters 12 to 14 must be held together and the scene depicted here needs to have chapter 12 as the backdrop to it. It describes the same event but from a different aspect. We again see all the nations united against Jerusalem. At first they inflict great harm (14:1–2). Then the Lord himself comes to fight in the battle on the side of Jerusalem. There follows a report of both sides in the conflict.

Peace for the people of God (14:3–9)

On the day Messiah places his feet on the Mount of Olives, an earthquake will form a new valley in the very place where the

Mount of Olives stood (verse 4). The Lord enters the city accompanied by the holy ones – angels and saints (verse 5), the physical environment changes (verses 6–8) and Messiah is crowned, whilst the uniqueness of his name will be universally recognized (verse 9).

The mountains will have been levelled to a plain, but Jerusalem will be in a commanding position above it. People return to the long awaited eternal peace and security of the city (verses 10–11).

Plague for the enemies of God (14:19)

There follows the judgment of the nations. They suffer the plague which will be Hiroshima-like (verses 12–15). Many die, but others survive only to suffer the consequences of the plague and the cruelty of their neighbours. Through it all there has obviously been a witness to the Messiah, for many survivors believe and join the worship of the Lord Almighty (verses 16–19).

The final picture reveals the total consecration of everything to the Lord. Paradise is restored and the king reigns (14:20–21).

What is Zechariah saying to us today through this apocalyptic language? To try to unravel all the mysteries is beyond the purpose of this book and I think is to miss the point of the prophecy. God's Kingdom is assured, but it will come through great tribulation. This is the message of Scripture; it is the message of experience too. Evil is the enemy of good and will do its utmost to destroy it, not only at the climax of the ages, but also at every point in time, wherever the powers of the kingdom assert themselves. To represent the kingdom and the powers of the kingdom, to live as citizens of the kingdom now, means to run the risk of violent opposition or even violent death. This can hardly come as a surprise, for the story of the gospel is that strength comes through weakness, victory comes through defeat, resurrection comes through crucifixion. The pattern of God's Kingdom, like the pattern of our salvation, is that of life through death, triumph through tribulation.

Nevertheless, it has to be said that the Lord Jesus ascended from the Mount of Olives and he told his disciples that he would return. The disciples, having witnessed the ascension are brought back to earth by the angels who said, 'Men of Galilee, why do you stand looking into the sky? This same Jesus, who has been taken from you into heaven, will come back in the same way you have seen him go into heaven' (Acts 1:11). The language leaves no room for misunderstanding. At some time in the future, the Lord Jesus will return to the earth. When he comes, all the prophecies concerning his righteous rule will be fulfilled in every detail. Lasting peace will prevail. Righteousness will reign, poverty will be abolished and harmony between individuals and nations will be established.

If Christ is not coming back, the prophets are false, the Bible is a confusing book, all Christians are deluded and God is untrue; but the Lord Jesus is coming back and every prediction of the Bible and every hope of the righteous will some day be realized.

His coming will involve the judgment of the living nations. Horrible though these things are, they are perfectly compatible with the teachings of Jesus (Matthew 25:32ff) and all the New Testament writers. A question that the New Testament writers leave us with is, 'Are you ready for that great day of the Lord?'

Saint Augustine wrote much about our Lord's return and discussed whether or not we should look for it as being imminent. He wrote beautifully,

> That day lies hid, that every day we may be on the watch. He who loves the coming of the Lord is not he who affirms that it is afar off, nor is it he that says that it is near; but rather he who, whether it be far off or near, awaits it with sincere faith, steadfast hope, and fervent love.

Questions

___

1. If you were to make a documentary film of verses 1–5 how would you depict the events described?
2. How should belief in the second coming of Christ affect the way that we live (2 Peter 3:11 and 1 John 2:3)?
3. When Jesus is king over all the earth, what will life be like? (Remember the principles of interpretation referred to in the introduction on pp. 21ff).

The Mount of Olives (14:3)

___

The Mount of Olives is a flattened, rounded ridge with four identifiable summits, named from the olive groves which, in ancient times covered it. It is something over a mile in length and forms the highest level of the range of hills to the east of Jerusalem (compare Zechariah 14:4 and Ezekiel 11:23), rising 77 metres (250 ft) higher than the temple mount and to 800 metres (2,600 ft) above sea level. Hence the supreme technical significance of the Mount of Olives demonstrated in the Roman siege of Jerusalem under Titus in AD 70. The Romans seemed to have named the northern extension of the ridge 'the look-out,' or Mount Scopus (cf. telescope), for this very reason. There are other Old Testament references to the Mount of Olives as in 2 Samuel 15:30, but the scene depicted in Zechariah 14:4 is apocalyptic in nature and it still awaits a clear explanation and fulfilment.

Historically the Mount of Olives finds its main interest in New Testament times, where it is a locality intimately connected with the Jerusalem ministry of Jesus Christ. It is important here to distinguish authentic history from the legendary accretions. Christ's first sight of the city on his triumphal entry was from the summit of the Mount of Olives (Luke 19:41), and his visits to the home of Mary, Martha and Lazarus in Bethany must have taken him frequently that way (Luke 21:37). The Mount was also the scene of his apocalyptic utterance inspired no doubt by the prospect of doomed Jerusalem from the mountain-side (Matthew 24:3, 25). Gethsemane was located somewhere on the Mount of Olives and it was certainly the site of the ascension (Acts 1:11–12).

The Feast of Tabernacles (14:16, 18)

The Feast of Tabernacles (or booths) was one of the most ancient of Israelite festivals, commemorating the season of harvest (compare Leviticus 23:24; Exodus 34:22 *etc.*). It had historical reference to the deliverance of Israel from Egypt and emphasized the belief that the life of the nation began and would continue under the redemptive care of God and each occasion of the feast was accompanied by the solemn reading of the Torah (the Book of the Law: compare Nehemiah 8:14–18). Its association specifically with rain, as referred to in verse 17, was not generally known until after the exile when water was brought from Siloam to Jerusalem (compare John 7:37).

Egypt (14:18, 19)

Egypt is used here representatively. It stands in this context for those nations or peoples who do not rely upon the Lord for their well-being and survival but rely upon 'natural' resources e.g., the flooding of the Nile (before the dams were built the annual flooding of the Nile was crucial for the growth of crops in the Nile Valley).

QUESTION TIME

Malachi 1:1 – 2:16

Malachi 1:1–5

Do you love me?

God loves us, but we feel quite often that he doesn't.

Introduction to Malachi

Malachi, evidently, was associated with the
work of Nehemiah. There is no mention of
Ezra or Nehemiah in his prophecy, nor of him in their writings.
However, from the conditions reflected in the book, it is usually
dated around 460–430 BC – the time of Nehemiah's ministry.

Furthermore, when we read the last chapter of Nehemiah's
book, we find that the sins of the people that angered Nehemiah
inspired the messages of Malachi. They include a corrupt
priesthood, the curse of inter-marriage and the failure to pay
their tithes. Malachi came to expose their sins, rebuke their
wrong attitudes and to challenge them to face up to the facts of
their special relationship with God. The real burden of
Malachi's prophecy, however, is to communicate God's love to
his people and his longing for them to be in that place where he
can bless them. Their response was one of incredulity. They
couldn't believe that Jehovah loved them and asked, 'How have
you loved us?'(1:2).

The question not only reveals the attitude of the people, but
also introduces us to the approach Malachi uses to convey his

message. The book is constructed around six questions (1:2; 1:6; 2:14; 2:17; 3:7; 3:13), with several secondary questions together with appropriate answers. All of the key questions were asked by way of a protest against the charges made in an initial theological statement. The whole prophecy reveals an insensitive people in conversation through the prophet, with a sensitive God. So Malachi begins with the revelation of God's love for his people, but the people just couldn't see it.

The quality of his love

'"I have loved you," says the Lord' (1:2). This was a burden of love. Our English language fails to convey adequately what is revealed here. The Hebrew tense implies continuity suggesting I have loved, I do love, I will love you (see Jeremiah 31:3).

Despite God's complaints, delivered through the prophet's messages, they had not affected the love of God. God's love showers on us as the rain, or shines on us as the sun, free and undeserved. It is completely unmerited on our part. There never was, and there never could be anything in us to attract God's affection, since we have deserved condemnation for our sinful disobedience and rebellion against him. In conferring his love on us, God has regard only to his own will and pleasure (Ephesians 1:5).

The truth that God's love is independent of merit is obvious by observing his dealings with his ancient people. It can also be a marvellous comfort, especially when we are aware of our sins. Our sins do not hinder God's love, but they do hinder our awareness of it. God corrects and chastens, but doesn't change his love – Hallelujah!

The question of his love

Why then did they feel so unloved as to ask, 'How have you loved us?' They were suffering economic hardships and persistent opposition from neighbours. Exiles returning from

Jerusalem to Susa, the capital of the Persian kings, reported to Nehemiah the terrible conditions in Jerusalem and Judah (Nehemiah 1:3). In all probability it was these conditions that caused them to question the love of God.

In answer, they were told to look at their brother nation Edom who had suffered disaster and would not recover. The verse, 'Yet I have loved Jacob, but Esau I have hated' (1:2), has been a problem to many Christians. This is not the place for a full discussion on divine election, but let it be said that God did not purpose sin in either of these men or peoples. They did not become what they were because God loved or hated. Rather, the demonstration of God's love for his people is seen here. Jacob and Esau had equal opportunity; both were sons of Isaac and therefore heirs of the promise, yet one was chosen and the other not chosen for God to display his purposes.

It should be said that the contrast between 'loved and hated' is a characteristically Hebrew way of describing loving selection and calling, rather than emotional feeling, so that the contrast may be (more naturally) one between 'specially chosen' and 'not specially chosen', rather than between elected and rejected. Nowhere in the Bible does it say Jacob was more worthy of God's love, or more lovable than Esau; but God's election and redeeming love was manifest towards him. God's election was made according to his own purpose (Ephesians 1:11). God did not wait to see how Jacob and Esau would turn out before he elected one of them. His own call was the decisive issue irrespective of worth. Jacob, chosen by the grace of God, was a deceiver and it was his robbing Esau of his birthright and blessing that caused so much of the antagonism between them and subsequently between the nations of Israel and Edom.

The fact was Israel enjoyed a unique relationship with Jehovah – he was their Lord, their father and their master (1:6) – and such a relationship must be reciprocal, but they were showing contempt for him. Malachi's burden was to see them return to a place of blessing, but there were conditions that had to be met and they will be seen in the following studies.

Questions

1. How can we be sure of God's love for us?
2. How does believing in the sovereignty of God affect the way that we share our faith with others? Are there disagreements in your church about election? Discuss the differences in love.
3. What happened to Edom? What appropriate response does the Lord expect from his people Israel (1:4–5)? What has this to say to us today?

Malachi

The name Malachi means 'My messenger'. Whether this is the real name of the prophet or simply a title is a matter of debate.

Edom

Edom was a nation whose people were the descendants of Esau, also called Edom. He founded the country, so his name is equated with it (Genesis 25:30; 36:1–8). The country was also called Seir, or Mount Seir, which was the name of the territory in which the Edomites lived; the mountain and plateau area between the Dead Sea and the Gulf of Aqabah was about 161 km (100 miles) long and up to 64 km (40 miles) wide (see map). The returned exiles bitterly resented the Edomites, who had joined with Babylon in the siege and destruction of Jerusalem in 589–587 BC.

Malachi 1:6–14

Do you respect me?

Carelessness in worship can close a church down.

The lack of blessing amongst God's people is not to be traced to a lack of love on God's part (1:2), but a lack of respect on the part of God's people (1:6). The respect that a son  offers a father, or a servant offers his master is not reflected in the Jewish priests' attitude towards Jehovah. Three specific charges are made.

- They cheated God by offering second best to him (2:7, 14).

- They showed contempt for the Lord's table by lack of consecration (2:7, 8).

- They were content at the state of affairs and needed to be stirred to the action of faith (2:9, 10).

They would not treat the local governor in the way they treated God and if they tried they would soon meet his displeasure (verse 8). To see what most of the governors were like, see Nehemiah 5:15.

Carelessness in worship and offering the Lord second best is still with us. Living sacrifices are still required (Romans 12:1–2); the offering of life itself, time, talents and treasures. This section challenges our Christian commitment. Nothing but the best is required of those who call themselves the people of God.

The significant consequence of this contempt of God revealed in the carelessness of worship is that the temple doors would be shut (1:10). Worship would move out from the temple to cover all the nations. Malachi may have had the dispersed Jews in mind but with the benefit of the New Testament, we know that it finds fulfilment in the spread of the church of Jesus Christ worldwide (1:11, 14). The conversation of Jesus with the woman at Sychar's well is a striking commentary on this passage (John 4).

The Jews in Malachi's time considered their worship to be a mere duty instead of a delight. It was all burdensome and they turned their noses up at the monotony of it all (1:12–13). The Lord cannot remain indifferent to such contempt.

Malachi's message to us is that worship embraces the whole of life. It is our thoughts and feelings of praise, wonder, sorrow and love for God, in his greatness and in his nearness. It includes things that we do together in a time of worship to express our thoughts and feelings. Worship, however, is also the action that we take to serve God and to share his love. The danger Malachi reveals is that it is possible for people to be so far from God in relationship that an act of worship becomes pointless. We can keep the old forms of worship in place for the sake of tradition. The Father is looking for those that will worship him 'in spirit and in truth' (John 4:23).

The call to repentance is once again present (1:9), but they will have to do more than 'Implore God to be gracious'. They need to improve their offerings. Grace is received by the action of God-given faith (Ephesians 2:8–10; James 2:17, 24).

Questions

Why not read this passage as a dramatized reading, one person taking Malachi's part and the rest of the group responding as the priest.

1. If we were to view the temple's sacrifices as referring to our

offerings of time, talents and treasures i.e., our commitment to Christ, what does it say to us about the quality of our offering?

2. What is good and helpful about your worship services and what might be done to make them even more meaningful?

3. Some commentators believe that verse 11 might refer to genuine worship of God taking place outside and beyond the community of the chosen people. What do you think about that?

Biblical sacrifices (1:7, 8)

The priests are accused of showing contempt for Jehovah, by offering blemished sacrifices. For the rules concerning the offering of animals see Exodus 12:5; Leviticus 1:3, 10; 22:18–25; Deuteronomy 15:21; *etc*.

The Lord's table (1:7, 12)

Malachi is the only one to use this particular phrase (but compare Psalm 23:5 and Ezekiel 44:16). The reference is to the altar itself, but probably also to the tables provided in the inner temple court for the slaughtering of sacrifices.

Malachi 2:1–9

Priests get it in the neck and face!

Spiritual leaders are answerable for the way they lead.

 The priests continued to be corrected, not only for what they had allowed to happen in worship, but for what they had not done i.e., communicated God's standard for the people as set out in the law (2:6–9).

The charge against them

They had violated their priestly calling in three specific ways:

▶ By refusing to listen to God's word or honour his name (2:2)

▶ By refusing to teach the truth of God's word (2:8)

▶ By refusing to be impartial before God's word (2:9).

The apostle James reminds us, 'We who teach will be judged more strictly' (James 3:1). This truth is born out by Malachi. The priests had position without divine power and they had a formalism without reality.

The chastening they faced

The price they had to pay for their spiritual neglect included:

▶ *A curse on their blessings* (2:2). The Lord would cause all that they considered to be blessings, i.e., material resources, to become a burden to them.

▶ *A rebuke on their descendants* (2:3). The effect of their sin would be felt by subsequent generations.

▶ *Dung on their faces* (2:3). The offal of the sacrificial animals had to be disposed of in a prescribed way (Exodus 29:14; Leviticus 4:11 *etc.*), but the priests were so disgusting that it would be spread on their faces.

In these ways, the Lord would humble the leaders and cause them to be despised before all the people (2:9).

The challenge before them

The whole purpose of this word of correction was to provide a better model for spiritual leadership. The priests were called back to basics and to recover what had been lost (2:4–7).

▶ To enter into a covenant relationship with the Lord and to experience life and peace (2:4–5). The word 'peace' here is 'shalom' which involves the idea of wholeness, prosperity, health and salvation.

▶ To stand in awe of God (2:5).

▶ To teach the word of God, resulting in many being converted (2:6).

The priests had failed because, instead of safe-guarding the truth entrusted to them (compare 2:7 and Jude 3), they had become ignorant and they had nothing to pass on to their people. What a solemn warning this is to Christian leaders in every age.

Questions

1. How important is a personal relationship with the Lord? How would you describe your relationship with him?
2. How can a church leader's walk with God affect the whole life of a congregation? From the passage before us what is required of church leaders?
3. How can we test what is taught in church to see if it is true or not?

'My covenant with Levi' (2:4 and 5)

This is an example of the Hebrew idea of corporate personality. Levi here represents the Tribe of Levi, or the Levites (Numbers 3:45; 18:21–24; Deuteronomy 33:8–11). It speaks of a special relationship with God, based on an agreement with promises. This covenant is described as 'a covenant of life and peace' (2:5). This expression appears only here in the Bible. To enter into covenant relationship with the Lord is to find the way to life in all its fullness. The covenant brings with it not only blessings, however, but responsibilities and these are spelt out in verse 5, in the terms 'reverence' and 'awe'.

Malachi 2:10–16

Why?

The Lord has strong feelings about marriage and divorce.

There is usually no answer to the 'Why?' question. In the face of suffering we all ask it. On this occasion, however, when the people asked, 'Why?', they had a very direct answer (2:14). The Lord was lovingly disciplining his people. The prophet charged the people with two sins.

Mixed marriages

In those days mixed marriages with partners of different faiths and nationalities were described as a 'terrible wickedness' and constituted 'being unfaithful to God' (Nehemiah 13:23–28). The magnitude of the sin arose from the fact that such behaviour was inconsistent with belonging to the covenant of their Father. The prophet is focusing on the nation as a family whose father is Jehovah. Not only has the special relationship with God been spoilt, but also special relationships which should exist in the community of faith (2:10, 14). The unity of the people is found in God who is both father and creator (compare Deuteronomy 32:6; Isaiah 63:16).

'Judah has desecrated the sanctuary the LORD loves by

marrying the daughter of a foreign god' (2:11). The real problem was not marrying someone of another nation, but of another religion, thereby compromising in the matter of worship.

A similar situation prevails when Christians marry non-Christians. Paul advised against it in the New Testament for the same reason as Malachi and Nehemiah (2:6–14). Experience still teaches that an unbeliever is more likely to pull a believer away from true discipleship, than for the opposite to happen. When children are born, often a real tension is experienced. The advice given is to give sin a wide berth.

Divorce

The other offence against God that Malachi addresses here is divorce. The exiles returning to Judah found life hard and the prospect of marrying into a prosperous non-Jewish family was attractive. Divorce was therefore a way of disposing of the hindrance to affording a new wife! This was a sin against God and the women involved (2:14). The Lord is the witness to the marriage covenant and he is holding them to their vows. Marriage is not simply a personal matter or just a social institution, it is 'God's chosen way for the continuance of mankind and the bringing up of children in security and trust'. Only when parents remain faithful to their marriage vows will God's desire for godly children be fulfilled (2:15). Divorce is called here a violent injustice and for these reasons God says, 'I hate divorce' (2:16).

Underlying both the two sins of mixed marriages and divorce is the offence of unfaithfulness to God, and Malachi concludes this message by repeating the phrase, 'Do not break faith' (2:15–16). The first call is to be faithful to your marriage partner, the second an open call to faithfulness. Faithfulness in relationships is what holds a family together. God is faithful, therefore people in a special relationship to him will be faithful also (Galatians 5:22).

Questions

1. What advice would you give to a Christian contemplating marriage to a non-Christian?
2. What priority do you think 'Marriage matters' should have in the ministry programme of churches? Why? How?
3. God may 'hate divorce' but what should be our attitude to those who are either facing divorce, or who have been divorced?

Divorce

In the Old Testament divorce was permissible (Deuteronomy 24:1–2). Re-marriage was also clearly acceptable. There was little else for a divorced woman to do. Jesus' statement in Matthew 5:31–32, that divorce is not to be allowed except for marital unfaithfulness, is not found in Mark's Gospel. It does seem to indicate the principle that if marriage is destroyed by unfaithfulness, it cannot be further destroyed by divorce. Jesus was being put to the test by a group of hostile Jews, who believed that only a woman could commit adultery, and Jesus there points out that a man can commit adultery too. He does not go further into the matter.

The Bible teaches the higher law of forgiveness even for the repentant adulterer (see Hosea). Paul speaks in 1 Corinthians 7:10–15 of a specific case involving marriage. He states that if an unbelieving partner leaves the marriage, the believer is no longer bound to them. This has led many to believe that Paul here is allowing for the re-marriage of the so-called innocent party.

It is clear from Malachi's prophecy that the Lord does hate divorce. It was never the Lord's intention to make divorce mandatory. It was only ever permitted because of the sinful nature of men and women (Matthew 19:1–9).

154

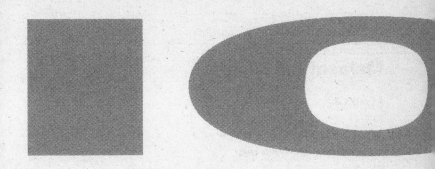

MORE
QUESTIONS

Malachi 2:17 – 4:6

Malachi 2:17 – 3:5

How?

Sin must be and will be judged.

The section opens with a clear statement, 'You have wearied the LORD with your words.' They couldn't see 'how' they had wearied him and asked for an explanation. The Lord graciously told them it was the way in which they questioned his justice (2:17).

The Jews of Malachi's day were faced with the problem with which the Old Testament writers often wrestled; how sinners got away with murder and seemingly, it was the good people who suffered most (compare Job 21:7–16; Habakkuk 1:2–4, 13). The assurance given is that the day of judgment is on its way and no-one will be able to withstand it (3:1–2). Two messengers are referred to, and two ways of dealing with the problem of sin.

The first messenger

He is described as 'my messenger'. This is a play on words. Malachi means 'My messenger', but whilst he did speak God's word, he is nevertheless referring to one who is to come. The New Testament writers agree unanimously that it was John the Baptist (Matthew 11:10; Mark 1:2; Luke 1:76). John's clear moral stand and his threat of God's judgment to be administered by Jesus (Luke 3:7–17) made him the rightful heir of the promise.

The messenger of the covenant

The second messenger is called 'the messenger of the covenant' who would come to his temple (3:1), and was to be fulfilled by the Lord himself. In his first coming to the earth, the Lord Jesus came to the temple and was recognized by Simeon (Luke 2:27). He came back to the temple at the age of twelve (Luke 2:49) and he returned many times until he rode into Jerusalem in triumph to cleanse the temple (Matthew 21:12–14). He came as the messenger of the covenant to secure peace between God and man.

The Lord Jesus still comes as we desire him (3:1), to cleanse and to purify us from our sin (3:2).

He is still to come in judgment, however, to fulfil this and other prophecies. As we have seen before, when the Old Testament prophets spoke about the coming of Christ, they could only see the fact that in a general sense he, the Messiah, would come. They probably thought in terms of one coming only; but as we compare scripture with scripture now, we can see that in actual fact they declared that Christ would come twice.

The twofold coming of Christ can be illustrated by the two metaphors provided in this passage. His coming is described both as a refiner's fire and a launderer's soap (3:2–3). The launderer's soap makes dirty clothes clean whilst the refiner's fire removes all the impurities from precious metals. These metaphors reveal the dual purpose of the coming of Christ. He comes both to cleanse the faithful and to eliminate the unfaithful.

All of those who have ever confessed their sin to God have known the joy of cleansing, but the refining process, the separating of the righteous from the unrighteous is still to be completed.

157

The one who will do the work of separation is the Lord himself and the object is to separate the dross from the gold and silver. All this will be done with patient love and unflinching justice.

Whilst Jesus was on earth there were manifestations of his glory that were too much for people to endure, such as the transfiguration, but when the Son of Man comes in all his glory, then no-one will be able to resist him. The final separation of sheep and goats will then take place (Matthew 25:31–32).

This word came originally to the priests of Malachi's day (1:6 and 2:1) and they would have understood that only when their morals were brought into line with God's righteousness, would their offerings in the temple be acceptable (3:4). Similarly we must hear that those responsible for social injustice sinned not only against people but against the Lord himself (3:5). Jesus himself said that social injustice would be the yardstick by which the judgment of the nations would take place on his final return (Matthew 25:34–46). What a solemn truth this is; God will judge us in accordance with our reaction to human need. His judgment does not depend on how clever we are, the popularity we enjoy or the fortune that we have earned, but rather on the help that we have given.

Questions

1. What are your feelings as you look forward to the day of judgment?
2. All forms of exploitation are condemned (3:5). What action is called for by individuals and churches to combat it in its various forms?
3. What good news for the world is there in this study?

The first and second comings of Christ

There are many scriptures that hold together the teaching of the first and the second coming of Christ. For example:

▶ Genesis 3:15. Here is a clear prophecy that Satan would strike the Saviour's heel. This he did at Calvary. But there is also the prophecy that Christ would crush Satan's head. This he will do when he comes again (compare 2 Thessalonians 2:8).

▶ Psalms 22 and 24. Psalm 22 is a prophecy of our Lord's first coming and of his suffering. Psalm 24 is a prophecy of the return of Jesus as the King of glory.

▶ Isaiah 61:1–2. Compare these two verses with Luke 4:18–19 and notice the significant fact that in quoting from Isaiah 61, our Lord left out the words 'And the day of vengeance of our God' for the simple reason that these words were not fulfilled at his first advent, but they will be fulfilled at his second.

▶ Matthew 16:21, 27. In verse 21 our Lord predicts his death upon Calvary; but verse 27 speaks of his coming 'In his Father's glory'.

▶ 1 Corinthians 11:23–26. Here the Apostle Paul gives us the instructions concerning the celebration of the Lord's supper, which points back to and is a reminder of our Lord's first coming, but points us forward to his second coming 'Until he comes'.

▶ Hebrews 9:24–28. Verse 26 refers to our Lord's first coming; verse 24 refers to his present work in heaven, while verse 28 is the promise of his second coming.

▶ Revelation 21 and 22. In Revelation 21 Jesus is referred to as the 'Lamb' which has special reference to his first coming, no less than seven times (Revelation 21:9, 14, 22, 23, 27; Revelation 22:1, 3). Then three times in Revelation 22 the Lord declares, 'Behold, I am coming soon!' (Revelation 22:7, 12, 20).

From these references we see something of the harmony of the prophetic word and the fact that throughout Scripture there is a clear testimony to the two comings of Christ that are implied by Malachi's prophecy.

Malachi 3:6–12

Will we rob God?

God loves a cheerful giver.

Malachi calls the people to genuine repentance which will demonstrate its reality by costly action. God's response to such repentance will be equally manifest.

The indictment laid against God's people is that they 'rob God' by failing to bring their tithes and offerings. The principle of giving to God is consistent and absolute throughout the Bible. When we give, God blesses, when we withhold, we put ourselves under a curse (3:9). The apostle Paul taught that there was blessing for generous givers (2 Corinthians 9:6–15). However, he was always careful to hold this prosperity theology firmly in tension with the theology of suffering (2 Corinthians 4:7–17). It should therefore be noticed that this word on giving is delivered not to givers but to withholders. The teaching can be summed up in a sentence: restore what you have stolen and stand back and see God blessing you beyond your wildest dreams.

Restore what you have stolen

The place of this restitution – the storehouse (3:10)

The storehouse had been built in the temple for depositing the tithes and offerings of the people (See Nehemiah 10:38–39 and compare Deuteronomy 14:22–29). One application which deserves careful consideration is as follows: the New Testament counterpart of this principle is the giving of all tithes to the local church. The local church will use the tithes and offerings to meet needs beyond the local church, but that is the place where they are to be brought. One of the greatest sins of our time is the robbing and defrauding of the local church by its members, and until such restitution is made, God cannot be pleased. This practice does not mean that we cannot give to other places, but our tithes need to be brought to the local church. Other giving should be as free-will offerings over and above the required tithes.

Another widely held view is that, since the New Testament does not bind Christians to tithe we are free to respond generously but not required to continue to obey the Old Testament law.

The proportion of this restitution – the whole tithe (3:10)

Tithing is 400 years older than the law. Abraham gave tithes to God through Melchizedek, the King-Priest (Genesis 14:17 – 15:1). Many Christians today interpret the Old Testament principles to mean that we should give 10% of our income. It is not to be thought of as a tax, but as a thank offering. We could never repay God for the love that he showers upon us. Tithing is a way of saying thank you to God for all that he has done for us.

It is for each Christian and for each congregation to decide whether tithing is an appropriate way ahead for their giving. In coming to a decision before God let none of us judge our neighbour for disagreeing with us.

The purpose of this restitution – That there may be food in my house (3:10)

Tithes and offerings were the priest's only means of support. In a similar way, God has ordained that the ministers today should live and function by means of their members' offerings (see 1 Corinthians 9:1–14). It is an indictment against the church in our land that too many ministers are discouraged. They are depressed and often under-paid. Many spouses have to go out to work to meet the necessities of life. May God give us grace to give sacrificially, not because it brings blessing, but because it is right to do so. Do it for the glory of God; do not give to get, but do it because God requires it. This is the right motive, acting upon a principle because it is right. However, God is on record as promising that when we give, we get (compare 3:10 and Luke 6:38).

Receive what God gives (3:10–12)

Just imagine God opening the floodgates of blessing. The Lord calls us to test him, or prove him in this matter of giving. This blessing includes:

The reviving of our fortunes (3:10)

This is a reversal of all that was wrong and still is wrong in our days: leaders of the church of God, living worthily of their calling; the house of the Lord honoured and attended, providing a sense of God in the land; the people of God enjoying holy marriages and strong family life. This is nothing less than revival described.

The rebuking of our foes (3:11–12)

The locust had eaten the crops and the mildew and blasting had destroyed what was left. These physical pests and the neighbouring nations represented the enemy of the people of God. Today they symbolize the forces of Satan that are arrayed against the church. Outside of the experience of being filled with the Spirit there is no authority to rebuke the devil and his minions, but once God breaks through from heaven, the enemy is rendered helpless and hopeless (see Isaiah 59:19 AV).

Questions

1. What do you understand by tithing? What proportion of our income belongs to the Lord?
2. How would your local church feel about 'testing' God in the way suggested? Why?
3. What is needed besides material prosperity for a country to be considered 'a delightful land' (3:12)?

Malachi 3:13 – 4:6

The sceptic's question

Good and evil will have its own reward.

'We've tried it and it does not work,' was the attitude of some who heard the Lord's call to test him in this matter of living righteously and giving generously (3:10). They reasoned, 'It is futile to serve God. What did we *gain* ...? .... but the evildoers *prosper* ...' (3:14–15). They had failed to understand that the prosperity theology must at all times be kept alongside the theology of suffering (Philippians 4:11–13).

A contrast is then made between the righteous and the wicked, with the implication that we are free to choose whether we serve God or not (3:16–18).

The future, however, not the past, will reveal the truth about God's justice. The faithful will be remembered and blessings bestowed, whilst the wicked will be destroyed.

The remembering of the faithful (3:16)

Amongst all the formalism and apostasy of Malachi's day, there remains a faithful remnant. Two things are said about this group. The first is that they 'talked with each other'. Literally it means that they made a constant habit of sharing together. There is a uniqueness about Christian fellowship that has its own inherent blessing and we impoverish ourselves by staying away from meeting with true believers.

The second thing we are told about this group is that they 'honoured his name'.

> Quite literally it means to take an inventory. These people thought upon the name. They were taking an inventory of their wealth in the name. The kings had gone, the priests were corrupt, the prophets were silent, but they still have the name. To them the name was Jehovah.
>
> (G. Campbell Morgan, *Voices of Twelve Hebrew Prophets* (Baker, 1975), pp. 158–159)

The revealing of the furnace (4:1)

Malachi describes here this day of the Lord in a twofold way. Towards the wicked it would be a day of burning destruction. Towards the righteous it would be a day when they would know the warmth of healing and of salvation. That will be the day of ultimate blessing for the people of God.

Malachi ends his prophecy, appropriately, both looking back and looking forward. In looking back, they are charged to remember the law which was intended to be a source of blessing. In looking forward, it is predicted that the prophet Elijah would appear before the day of the Lord. In keeping with this text, at every Passover meal observed by Orthodox Jews, a cup of wine is poured for Elijah. The New Testament, however, sees John the Baptist as fulfilling this role (Luke 1:17; Matthew 11:10, 13–14; 17:10–13). Malachi, therefore, ends with an eye to the future and the coming of Messiah, when families will live in harmony.

This hope that is set before us is no mere escape mechanism to evade the real issues of life on this earth. On the contrary, it is a hope that takes seriously life and death and is afraid of neither. It is a hope that gives to human life, and the life of the universe, a meaning and a goal such as atheism or agnosticism can never do. It is a hope that affirms that life is worth living and our work, however apparently futile it may appear to be, is not in vain in the Lord.

Questions

1. What is there in the Christian faith that you are sceptical about? Why?
2. In what specific practical ways can you express a proper fear of the Lord and reverence for his name (3:16)?
3. Upon what attitude and actions is the division between the righteous and the wicked based (3:18; 4:1, 2)? See also Genesis 15:6.

For further reading

James Ayre, *In That Day* (Myrtle Vale Specialist Publishers, 1986).

Leslie Allen, *Bible Study Commentary, Hosea-Malachi* (SU/SLC, 1987).

Joyce G. Baldwin, *Haggai, Zechariah and Malachi. Tyndale Old Testament Commentary* (IVP, 1972).

Peter C. Craigie, *The Daily Study Bible, Twelve Prophets Volume 2* (The Saint Andrew Press, 1985).

Walter A. Elwell (editor), *Evangelical Dictionary of Theology* (Marshall Pickering, 1994).

Eugene H. Merrill, *An Historical Survey of the Old Testament* (The Craig Press, 1966).

Thomas V. Moore, *Haggai & Malachi* (Banner of Truth Trust, 1968).

Thomas V. Moore, *Zechariah* (The Geneva Series of Commentaries).

J. Dwight, *Pentecost, Things to Come* (Zondervan, 1971).

ACTS

Stephen Gaukroger

Free to live

Crossway Bible Guides

Series Editor for the New Testament: Ian Coffey

Acts is one of the most exciting and relevant Bible books for Christians today. It shows us God powerfully at work in the early church.

This invaluable study guide enables us to find out how Acts speaks to us now. There is plenty of application, so that we can put into practice the lessons we learn in each study.

The Crossway Bible Guides are specially designed for home-group study and for readers at all levels of ability.
Each section has:
   A detailed explanation of the passage
   Questions for group and personal study.

Some sections also have special features that explain complex passages in greater depth.

Stephen Gaukroger is one of Britain's best-known speakers, and the author of bestsellers such as *It Makes Sense*. The Senior Minister of a church in Bedfordshire, he was the youngest ever elected President of the Baptist Union. He and his wife Janet have three children.

EPHESIANS

Stephen Motyer

Free to be one

Crossway Bible Guides

Paul urges the Ephesian church to be at one; to be a place:

- ⋆ of strength for spiritual warfare
- ⋆ where relationships are transformed by God's grace and peace
- ⋆ where wholeness of living is vibrantly expressed

Crossway Bible Guides are designed for personal devotion and for group study leaders and members. They give a concise summary and lively application of each passage. They help us grasp the message of the Bible, and, more important, help the Bible get a grip on us.

A useful resource for personal Bible reading and group studies –
Michael Green

Evangelical Alliance is delighted to join together with Crossway in publishing this new series –
Clive Calver

Individuals or groups could find great benefit from this series. Major points are highlighted followed by uncompromising and sharp questions –
Donald English

These guides will facilitate, stimulate and enrich your discovery of God's Word –
Roger Forster

Steve Motyer taught at Oak Hill College and spent four years as a country vicar before becoming a lecturer in New Testament at London Bible College in 1987. He is a respected speaker, and author of *Israel in the Plan of God* and *Unlocking the Bible* (S.U.). He lives in Watford with his wife Val, their three children and a collection of tropical fish.

EZRA & NEHEMIAH

Dave Cave

Free to build

Crossway Bible Guides

The books of Ezra and Nehemiah are powerful examples of God's care for his people. His equipping of leaders for his people is as vital and dynamic today as in Old Testament times. We see how

* ★ leading in God's way brings lasting results
* ★ obeying God restores his blessing
* ★ trusting God defeats the opposition

Crossway Bible Guides are designed for personal devotion and for group study leaders and members. They give a concise summary and lively application of each passage. They help us grasp the message of the Bible, and, more important, help the Bible get a grip on us.

A useful resource for personal Bible reading and group studies –
                                                            Michael Green

Evangelical Alliance is delighted to join together with Crossway in publishing this new series –   Clive Calver

Individuals or groups could find great benefit from this series. Major points are highlighted followed by uncompromising and sharp questions –
                                                            Donald English

These guides will facilitate, stimulate and enrich your discovery of God's Word –   Roger Forster

Dave Cave is the leader of Anfield Road Fellowship, near Liverpool football stadium. A Spring Harvest and much-used conference speaker and radio broadcaster, he and his wife Tina live with their family in inner-city Liverpool.

HOUSEGROUPS

the leaders' survival guide

Editors: Ian Coffey and Stephen Gaukroger

Ever since New Testament times small groups of Christians have met to learn, to worship and to grow together. Housegroups have enjoyed great popularity in the last few decades, and much experience and wisdom in leading them has been distilled by the authors of this book.

Are you thinking of starting a housegroup or taking your existing group forward? Or has your group gone a little flat? *Housegroups: the leaders' survival guide* will give you the vision you are looking for:

- ★ What's the point of housegroups?
- ★ What makes a good leader?
- ★ Teaching the Bible in small groups
- ★ Prayer, worship and evangelism
- ★ Troubleshooter's guide and much more

Authors include Peter Meadows, John Earwicker, Dave Cave, Steve Motyer, Nick Mercer, Chris Bowater.

Editors Stephen Gaukroger and Ian Coffey are both senior ministers in Baptist churches and series editors of the Crossway Bible Guides. They share with the other authors a contagious enthusiasm for housegroups.

ISAIAH

Philip Hacking

Free to suffer and to serve

Crossway Bible Guides

Isaiah wrote to rulers and to people from all walks of life:

* ★ calling them back from a life of self-gratification
* ★ warning them of the consequences of disobedience
* ★ convincing them of God's glorious promises

Centuries have passed but conditions and attitudes are often strikingly similar today. These studies in Isaiah help us to focus on the essentials of daily living in the light of a sure bright hope for tomorrow.

Crossway Bible Guides are designed for personal devotion and for group study leaders and members. They give a concise summary and lively application of each passage. They help us grasp the message of the Bible, and, more important, help the Bible get a grip on us.

A useful resource for personal Bible reading and group studies –

Michael Green

Evangelical Alliance is delighted to join together with Crossway in publishing this new series –

Clive Calver

Individuals or groups could find great benefit from this series. Major points are highlighted followed by uncompromising and sharp questions –

Donald English

These guides will facilitate, stimulate and enrich your discovery of God's Word –

Roger Forster

Philip Hacking is Vicar of Christ Church, Fulwood, Sheffield, UK, and is a widely respected author and conference speaker, particularly at Spring Harvest, Word Alive and the Keswick Convention.

JOSHUA

Charles Price

Free to follow

Crossway Bible Guides

Joshua is a book about God! He is revealed as a God of action in the cut and thrust of real life. Joshua shows God:

- ★ dealing with real conflict
- ★ undergirding real disappointment
- ★ restoring after real failure
- ★ operating in real people

From Joshua we learn not only that God is indispensable; he is available to those who are available to him and follow him.

Crossway Bible Guides are designed for personal devotion and for group study leaders and members. They give a concise summary and lively application of each passage. They help us grasp the message of the Bible, and, more important, help the Bible get a grip on us.

A useful resource for personal Bible reading and group studies –   Michael Green

Evangelical Alliance is delighted to join together with Crossway in publishing this new series –   Clive Calver

Individuals or groups could find great benefit from this series. Major points are highlighted followed by uncompromising and sharp questions –   Donald English

These guides will facilitate, stimulate and enrich your discovery of God's Word –   Roger Forster

Charles Price is an experienced Bible teacher with a ministry that takes him all over the world. He is based at Capernwray Hall in Lancashire, where he lives with his wife Hilary.

LEVITICUS

Derek Tidball

Live as God's craftsmanship

Crossway Bible Guides

The book of Leviticus contains a dazzling collection of gems of truth, embedded in the God-centred society of old Israel. Mined, polished and displayed by an expert, their lustre is as appropriate for our culture as it was in their original Old Testament setting. We, too, are God's craftsmanship. This book encourages us to live in the light of that truth.

Leviticus majors on the two great commandments:

* ★ Love the Lord your God (chapters 1–16)
* ★ Love your neighbour as yourself (chapters 17–27)

Crossway Bible Guides are tailor-made for group study leaders and members and are also ideal for personal devotional use. They provide a concise summary and lively application of each passage, with pointed questions to probe more deeply into personal, church-centred and global issues. They help us to grasp the Bible's message and the Bible to get a grip on us.

A useful resource for personal Bible Reading and group studies –
                                                             Michael Green

Evangelical Alliance is delighted to join together with Crossway in publishing this new series –   Clive Calver

Individuals or groups could find great benefit from this series. Major points are highlighted followed by uncompromising and sharp questions –
                                                             Donald English

These guides will facilitate, stimulate and enrich your discovery of God's Word –   Roger Forster

Derek Tidball is Principal of London Bible College, Formerly Senior Minister of Mutley Baptist Church, Plymouth, and Head of the Mission Department of the Baptist Union of Great Britain, he is also a respected author and Bible expositor.

1 PETER

Andrew Whitman

Free to hope

Crossway Bible Guides

The apostle Peter encourages us to have hope in all circumstances
because

* ⋆ God's love for us is sure
* ⋆ God is always in control
* ⋆ God is in charge of the future

Crossway Bible Guides are designed for personal devotion and for
group-study leaders and members. They give a concise summary
and lively application of each passage. They help us grasp the
message of the Bible, and more important, help the Bible get a grip
on us.

A useful resource for personal Bible reading and group studies –
                                                    Michael Green

*Evangelical Alliance is delighted to join together with Crossway in
publishing this new series –*   Clive Calver

*Individuals or groups could find great benefit from this series. Major
points are highlighted followed by uncompromising and sharp
questions –*   Donald English

*These guides will facilitate, stimulate and enrich your discovery of
God's Word –*   Roger Forster

**Andrew Whitman is the pastor of Godmanchester
Baptist Church, near Huntingdon, where he lives with
his family.**

PSALMS 1–72

Alan Palmer

Worship your maker

Crossway Bible Guides

The book of Psalms has made an enormous impact on God's people. Psalms are frequently quoted in later books of the Bible and have formed the backbone of worship in the Christian church.

* ★ Psalms are the great hymnbook of the people of God.
* ★ They express a wide range of emotions and experiences.
* ★ Psalms offer us today a direct relationship with God.

Crossway Bible Guides are tailor-made for group study leaders and members and are also ideal for personal devotional use. They provide a concise summary and lively application of each passage, with pointed questions to probe more deeply into personal, church-centred and global issues. They help us to grasp the Bible's message and the Bible to get a grip on us.

A useful resource for personal Bible Reading and group studies –
Michael Green

Evangelical Alliance is delighted to join together with Crossway in publishing this new series –
Clive Calver

Individuals or groups could find great benefit from this series. Major points are highlighted followed by uncompromising and sharp questions –
Donald English

These guides will facilitate, stimulate and enrich your discovery of God's Word –
Roger Forster

Alan Palmer is Director of Oak Hill Extension College in North London. A graduate of the London Bible College, he has pastored churches in Canada and the UK.

TIMOTHY AND TITUS

Michael Griffiths

Train for discipleship

Crossway Bible Guides

Paul wrote twice to Timothy and once to Titus, equipping them to:

* make true disciples
* detect and eliminate false teaching
* appoint and encourage church elders and overseers
* clarify the roles of men and women in leadership

The problems which often face our churches today are strikingly similar to those met in first-century Ephesus and Crete. These letters were written for us.

Crossway Bible Guides are tailor-made for group study leaders and members and are also ideal for personal devotional use. They provide a concise summary and lively application of each passage, with pointed questions to probe more deeply into personal, church-centred and global issues. They help us to grasp the Bible's message and the Bible to get a grip on us.

A useful resource for personal Bible Reading and group studies –
Michael Green

Evangelical Alliance is delighted to join together with Crossway in publishing this new series –
Clive Calver

Individuals or groups could find great benefit from this series. Major points are highlighted followed by uncompromising and sharp questions –
Donald English

These guides will facilitate, stimulate and enrich your discovery of God's Word –
Roger Forster

Michael Griffiths is a widely respected conference speaker and author who, like Timothy, delights in making disciples. A former Director of the Overseas Missionary Fellowship and Principal of London Bible College, he is now a freelance Christian lecturer and writer.